Clarence R. Skinner

Clarence R. Skinner
1881-1949

Portrait by Joseph B. Cahill, 1948

Clarence R. Skinner
Prophet of a New Universalism

———◆———

Edited by Charles A. Howe

with James D. Hunt,
Alan L. Seaburg,
and Carl G. Seaburg

A Project of the Murray Grove Association

Skinner House Books
Boston

Printed in the USA.

ISBN 1-55896-374-X

10 9 8 7 6 5 4 3 2 1
02 01 00 99

Acknowledgments

"What is Worship" originally appeared in *Worship and the Well Ordered Life*
by Clarence R. Skinner, published 1955 by the Universalist Historical
Society and Meeting House Press. Reprinted by permission of Clarise L.
Patton.

"Clarence Skinner: Building a New Kind of Church" orginally appeared in
To Bring More Light and Understanding, The John Murray Distinguished
Lectures, Volume II, edited by Charles Howe, publised 1995 by the Murray
Grove Association. Reprinted by permission of the Murray Grove Associa-
tion.

Contents

Preface

Although Clarence R. Skinner is widely regarded as the most important American Universalist of the first half of the twentieth century, the details of his life and thought are for the most part inaccessible to today's general reader. The present volume is designed to help correct this deficiency and, in the process, to rescue Skinner from the dangers of both being forgotten and being honored in ignorance, without an adequate basis for judging the degree of importance he warrants. To achieve this, representative selections from his writings are included, with a bibliography of publications by and about Skinner, a biographical essay, and two critical articles assessing his contributions. No adequate biographical treatment of Skinner has previously been published, and the two critical articles are the first substantive analyses of Skinner as a theologian and an innovative ecclesiastic to appear.

The writings of Clarence R. Skinner have been selected and annotated by James D. Hunt, a former faculty member of the Crane Theological School at Tufts University, who is widely recognized as the foremost authority on Skinner's thought. Essays about Skinner were contributed by myself, James D. Hunt, and Carl Seaburg. The bibliography was compiled and updated by Alan Seaburg, former Curator of Manuscripts at the Andover-Harvard Library of Harvard Divinity School. Like Hunt, Alan Seaburg is a former faculty member of the Crane Theological School. Hunt and the two Seaburgs studied at Crane and were all ordained into the Universalist ministry prior to the Unitarian-Universalist merger; I am a retired Unitarian Universalist minister. With Charles A. Gaines, another Crane student, the five of us constitute the Murray

Grove Skinner Book Committee and have collaborated in the preparation of this volume, which is published under the joint auspices of Skinner House Books and the Murray Grove Association.

The cooperation of the staff of Skinner House Books, its project editor, Brenda Wong, and its managing editor, Patricia Frevert, and the support of the Board of Directors of the Murray Grove Association for the years 1992 to 1996 and its president, Rudolph Nemser, are acknowledged with deep thanks. We particularly appreciate the generous contribution from Cynthia B. Foster, a former parishioner of Skinner and a long-time member of the Community Church of Boston, which made publication of this volume possible. I wish to acknowledge my deep appreciation and indebtedness to Charles A. Gaines, whose thesis, "Clarence R. Skinner: Image of a Movement," provided most of the background material and sources for my essay, "Clarence R. Skinner: Prophet of a New Universalism," some of which would otherwise have been lost forever.

Charles A. Howe
Raleigh, North Carolina
March 1997

Chronology

1881	Born, Brooklyn, New York
1900-04	Student, St. Lawrence University (BA degree)
1904-06	Assistant to Frank Oliver Hall, Minister, Church of Divine Paternity, New York City
1906	Ordained to Universalist ministry
1906-11	Minister, Universalist Church, Mount Vernon, New York
1910	MA degree, St. Lawrence University
1910-19	Secretary, Commission on Social Service, Universalist General Convention
1911-14	Minister, Grace Universalist Church, Lowell, Massachusetts
1914-33	Professor of Applied Christianity, Crane Theological School, Tufts University
1915	*The Social Implications of Universalism* published
1917-19	Part-time minister, Medford Hillside Universalist Church
1920-36	Leader, Community Church of Boston
1931-41	Contributing editor, *Unity*
1931	*A Free Pulpit in Action* published
1933-45	Dean, Tufts School of Religion, Crane Theological School
1937	*Liberalism Faces the Future* published
1939	*Human Nature and the Nature of Evil* published
1941	*Hell's Ramparts Fell* published
1945	*A Religion for Greatness* published
1949	Died, Long Ridge, Connecticut
1955	*Worship and a Well Ordered Life* published

1959   Clarence R. Skinner Award established
1962   Skinner House acquired, dedicated at the Unitarian
        Universalist Association headquarters
1976   Skinner House Books imprint adopted by the Uni-
        tarian Universalist Association

The Life of a
Prophet

⬥

Three essays comprise this introduction to the life and work of Clarence R. Skinner. The biographical essay, "Clarence R. Skinner: Prophet of a New Universalism," by Charles A. Howe, is based largely on "Clarence R. Skinner: Image of a Movement," an unpublished thesis written by Charles A. Gaines between 1960 and 1961 and now archived at the Harvard Divinity School library. Gaines's sources include interviews with Skinner's widow, Clara.

James D. Hunt is the author of "The Liberal Theology of Clarence R. Skinner," republished from the 1967-1968 issue of *The Annual Journal of the Universalist Historical Society*. This article is a revised version of an address delivered to the Unitarian and Universalist Historical Societies in Miami, Florida, on May 16, 1966.

"Clarence Skinner: Building a New Kind of Church" is by Carl Seaburg, one of Skinner's students at Crane Theological School in the 1940s. The essay was delivered as the John Murray Distinguished Lecture in Fort Worth, Texas, on June 26, 1994, and previously appeared in *To Bring More Light and Understanding*, the second volume of the Murray lectures.

Clarence R. Skinner:
Prophet of a New Universalism

Charles A. Howe

Clarence Russell Skinner was born in Brooklyn, New York, on March 23, 1881, the son of Charles Montgomery Skinner and Ada Blanchard Skinner. His father, a newspaper editor long associated with the *Brooklyn Eagle*, was an individualist with broad and deep interests—in the arts (especially drama and literature), in nature (he was a competent amateur naturalist and an admirer of Emerson and Thoreau), and in social issues (he wrote a series of articles on such topics as "Workers and Trusts" and "Studies in Applied Socialism"). He was a prolific writer; in addition to numerous newspaper articles, he was the author of nine books and three plays. Taken together, his writings reflect a love of nature and a progressive social idealism. Charles Skinner was described "as having a well-developed New England conscience with an acute scrupulosity in regard to money and personal obligations," and his influence on his son was enduring and great. The influence of young Clarence's mother is difficult to judge. She was remembered as a loving woman who worked hard to maintain a dependable home environment in their Brooklyn apartment, and apparently she succeeded. The couple had three sons—Clarence, Harold, and Lindley, the latter dying while still young.

Nature walks, books, and theater were central to family life. Most of the walks were of necessity taken in nearby parks, but vacations in Vermont provided variety. Children's books were never read to Clarence as a boy; instead, he was raised on Plato and Whitman. Clarence's uncle Otis and cousin Cornelia Otis were two of the country's best-known actors, and thus the family never lacked for complimentary tickets to the theater. As a result of this rich exposure, Clarence seriously considered acting as a career, a course which Harold did follow.[1]

Clarence attended public schools in Brooklyn until during his high school years his difficulty with mathematics prompted his father to transfer him to Erasmus Hall, one of the leading preparatory schools in the area. Its principal was Walter B. Gunnison, a progressive, liberal educator who ran the school like a small college, an atmosphere in which young Clarence blossomed, becoming editor of the school newspaper and a member of the debating team and dramatic society; in addition, he attended the Pratt Institute on Saturdays, studying art and the sciences. While he was attending Erasmus, Clarence met Louis Pink; the two quickly established a close friendship that lasted until Clarence's death fifty years later. In 1900 they enrolled together in the freshman class of St. Lawrence University in Canton, New York.[2]

Almond Gunnison, Walter's brother, had been named president of the university the previous year, coming to St. Lawrence after a successful pastorate at the All Souls Universalist Church in Brooklyn where the Skinners were members. The university had been established by Universalists in 1856 and included both a nonsectarian liberal arts college and a small denominational theological school. Clarence's grandfather, Charles A. Skinner, had been a Universalist minister; so had his great grandfather, Warren Skinner, and his great uncle, Otis A. Skinner. Thus Clarence was raised in a pervasive climate of the Universalist tradition.[3]

College years were a time of further growth. Clarence continued his interests in dramatics and journalism, in time becoming president of the dramatic society and editor of the college newspaper. He was a good student, developing an especially keen interest in physics and foreign languages; in his senior year, when the German professor became ill, Clarence took over the teaching of the courses. In addition, he was elected class president and to membership in Phi Beta Kappa. Even more importantly, during his senior year Clarence Skinner fell in love and became engaged. Clara Louise Ayres was a classmate, and the two seem to have been drawn to each other by their similar personalities. Both were shy, studious, serious, and smart; Clara, too, was elected to Phi Beta Kappa—in fact she ranked second in the graduating class of forty, while Clarence ranked fourth. Clara was from a wealthy family; her father was a highly successful real estate investor from Stamford, Connecticut. She had led a sheltered life and her parents initially opposed the engagement, but after meeting Clarence they relented.[4]

The young couple were separated during the summer following graduation, with Clara going on a trip to Europe while Clarence stayed at his grandfather's home in Proctorsville, Vermont, reading, studying, and recovering from what was described as a minor nervous breakdown. That fall he became assistant to Frank Oliver Hall, minister of the Church of the Divine Paternity (now known as the Fourth Universalist Society) on Central Park West in Manhattan, one of the largest and most prestigious churches in the denomination. Given Clarence's academic background, it was a surprising move, for his interest in theology and the ministry had seemed marginal. He had taken a few courses at the theological school and preached a few times at the Canton Universalist Church while Clara played the organ, but the indications were that he planned to follow a career in acting. Perhaps now that he was engaged he realized that such a career would inevitably separate him too much from Clara.[5]

Clarence's title as assistant to Hall was taken quite literally by the latter. Hall was a somewhat dictatorial, blunt man who made it quite clear that his new assistant should not assume any roles that might conflict with his own. The roles he assigned to Clarence were those of youth leader, executive secretary, and general errand boy; on one occasion he was ordered to buy a sled for Hall to give to his daughter for Christmas. Once, when Hall was ill, Clarence filled the pulpit for an entire month; the *Brooklyn Eagle* gave his sermons good reviews and predicted a promising future for the fledgling preacher.[6]

Meanwhile, Clara, with her family's help, was preparing herself for her new role. She moved with her parents to Brooklyn that winter so that she could be close to Clarence, and she took courses in cooking, sewing, and dressmaking. The couple were able to spend much time together, often attending plays, operas, and the symphony; it was a busy, happy year, full of anticipation. On April 8, 1906, Clarence Russell Skinner was ordained to the Christian ministry at the Church of the Divine Paternity with Frank Oliver Hall preaching the ordination sermon. Clarence's relationship with Hall had been a valuable one and would continue for many years, but he felt ready to go out on his own.[7]

That summer Clarence received and accepted a call from the Universalist Church in Mt. Vernon, not far north of New York City. It was a small church, typical of those in which new ministers were settled—perhaps three dozen families, a signed-on membership of thirty, with forty children enrolled in the church school. The building was somewhat dilapidated, but the salary of $66 a month was considered quite good for someone just starting out. Moreover, Clara's parents were pleased that she would be staying so close to home. The wedding took place in Stamford on October 16 with Hall officiating before a small family gathering. After a honeymoon in Washington, the newlyweds moved into a new four-room apartment in Mt. Vernon. They were seldom apart for the next forty-three years.[8]

The five years in Mt. Vernon were busy ones. Clarence took on his ministerial tasks with enthusiasm, maintaining a rigorous self-imposed schedule that included a weekly quota of parish calls, for despite his shyness he considered these calls to be an essential part of his responsibility. All the administrative work of the parish fell on his shoulders, and the skills developed during his two years at Divine Paternity stood him in good stead. He was a gifted preacher, though initially his sermons were too idealistic and cluttered with overly long words; but his idealism soon became tempered by worldly realities, and his use of long words was minimized by Clara's criticisms—she was determined that his parishioners would understand what he was saying. The hard work paid off— church membership more than doubled, as did enrollment in the church school. It was not long before Clarence's work was attracting attention within the denomination, as evidenced by the following account in the *Universalist Leader*:

> The Rev. C. R. Skinner has recently declined a tempting call to one of our best churches. He knows that the work in Mt. Vernon is really just begun, and he feels that he cannot think of leaving it. He has made a real place for himself in that growing community, and is sure to have one of the best congregations in our Zion. We are all glad that Mt. Vernon is not to lose him. The Ladies' Aid Society raised nearly 1000 dollars the past year. The Crusaders are growing in numbers. They have added to their ranks a bugler, drummer and fife player. The Sunday School is nearing the 100 mark in registration. Mr. Skinner's series of sermons on "The Life of Christ in the Light of Modern Knowledge" has been attracting many strangers and edging them perceptibly toward Universalism.[9]

For Clara, the adjustment to a new life was difficult at first. Clarence was so fully occupied with his new work that the couple had little time together, and she was undoubtedly lonely. She was often ill, and her mother spent some time in Mt. Vernon nursing her. One of the few bright spots in her life was attending symphony concerts in New York City; Clarence had managed to get her a season ticket. Eventually she regained her health and adjusted to her new life. She accompanied Clarence on his out-of-town speaking engagements, usually driving their car, and found a role in the parish as the minister's wife. The couple never had children, and though they sometimes considered adoption, action was always postponed to a quieter time that never came.[10]

One of Clarence's major achievements at Mt. Vernon was the construction of a new church building. Early in his ministry he had invited his uncle Otis to speak at a Sunday service. Otis Skinner's fame as an actor attracted an overflow congregation, and the old building creaked and groaned so badly under the weight that Clarence feared it might collapse. To convince the small congregation that a new building was needed and to raise the necessary money ($82,000) was a major accomplishment, but the effort succeeded. The new church was dedicated on Easter Sunday, 1910, with a full congregation on hand. Mrs. Andrew Carnegie, a member of the Church of the Divine Paternity, had taken a great interest in the project and the money for a new organ was raised through a campaign in which she matched each contribution.[11]

Also in 1910 Clarence Skinner completed the requirements for a Master of Arts degree from St. Lawrence by taking course work at Columbia University; it was the last of his two earned degrees, neither in theology. At about this same time he came to a pacifist position, as evidenced by his articles in the *Universalist Leader.* "Why Not a Peace Day?" called on the churches to take leadership in establishing such a national holiday; another article, "Militarism or Christianity?," set forth the arguments against American militarism and called for a church organization to oppose it. Skinner was never to retreat from his pacifist position, even though it later brought him under strong attack. At about this time he was instrumental in forming a New York City area ministers' group that later evolved into the Church Peace Union, an organization that worked for peace by supporting the League of Nations and combating anti-Semitism.[12]

During his two years at Divine Paternity, Clarence Skinner often had taken part in the activities of the University Settlement House on the East Side, a project with which his friend Louis Pink had become involved following graduation from St. Lawrence. Clarence was attracted to this kind of social work and after settling in Mt. Vernon began making weekly trips to the city to continue his involvement in the project. Through this experience Clarence came to realize that, while settlement houses were valuable, their overall long-term impact was marginal and that a more basic approach, designed to address the root causes of social problems, was necessary. Walter Rauschenbush's *Christianity and the Social Crisis* had appeared in 1907; the Social Gospel movement in American churches was well under way; and it would not be long before Skinner would accept and expand its ideas. His mentor, Frank Oliver Hall, had made a powerful speech in 1909 at the Universalist General Convention urging that churches accept the responsibility for addressing the social problems of the times. Hall had long been concerned about the churches' role in such matters and helped establish a settlement house in New York City and a rural vacation center for underprivileged children; in addition, he was the author of a book, *Common People,* in which he outlined a program by which churches might help those caught up in the economic pressures of the day. As a direct result of his address, a denominational Commission on Social Service was established with Hall as its chair. Skinner was appointed as the commission's secretary, probably on Hall's recommendation; he was to serve in that capacity for a decade, making a major contribution to its work.[13]

In the spring of 1911, Skinner accepted an invitation to candidate for the ministry of Grace Universalist Church in Lowell, Massachusetts, a church considerably stronger and with greater opportunities for community service than that at Mt. Vernon. Early that summer a call was extended and he accepted. The couple stored their furniture in Stamford and enjoyed a well-earned vacation before moving to a new church, a new city, and a new challenge.[14]

Grace Church had a constituency of about 145 families, about 120 official members, and a church school enrollment of 150 children. It was located in the downtown area of a rapidly growing city, one of two thriving Universalist churches in Lowell. Clarence sensed vitality in both the churches and the city. The couple moved into rented quarters for the first year, then into a parsonage purchased by the church. As reported in the *Universalist Leader*, the church year got off to a fine start:

> The pastor, Rev. Clarence R. Skinner, is giving a series of sermons Sunday mornings on "The New Religion." The series consists of seven sermons running from October 8th to November 19th inclusive, in which as many aspects of the important subject will be treated. Beginning last Sunday evening, with an address by Dr. Perkins of Lynn, a series of evening services will be continued regularly for some weeks. At these meetings vital questions now confronting the American people will be discussed.[15]

The evening series, named the Lowell Forum, was an immediate success. On most occasions the church, which seated between four and five hundred people, was full. The program consisted of a short worship service, a collection to help cover expenses, and then an address by the evening's speaker, followed by discussion. The forum was based on a well-thought-out philosophy, and the time for such an innovation was ripe. As Skinner later wrote to Jane Addams of Chicago's Hull House, "It is tragic to witness the almost universal passion of the religious element of this country to serve the cause of a moral reformation in social life, and to see how ineffective that passion is because of the lack of definite channels of action."[16] The forum, Skinner believed, provided a model of how a church might become an effective agent for change without sacrificing its traditional function of worship. He wrote,

Men cannot live a completely spiritual life until all the forces which mould life are spiritualized. The Church Forum is an attempt to extend the inspiration and interpretation of religion. It tries to bring the world into the church and to carry the church out into the world. It establishes the long lost point of contact between spiritual and social forces. Its aim is to Christianize the Social Order.

The Problem which the Forum rouses is not one of subtraction, but of addition. It is not proposed that the distinctive function of the church shall be abandoned or that we shall substitute somewhat for its worship. But in the spirit of him who said, "I come not to be ministered unto but to minister," it is proposed that we shall add to its time-honored usage a new opportunity for the extension of its services.[17]

The goal of such a forum was, in Skinner's mind, to help build a religious democracy concerned with social betterment by bringing together "diverse and frequently antagonistic elements of population" so that unity could be achieved through a search for truth. The truth, he firmly believed, "will set us free from our petty provincialisms and narrow class interpretations." Accordingly, a rich variety of speakers with differing viewpoints were invited to address the forum. The schedule for January 1914 was typical:

January 4: "The Superman," Mr. John Cowper of Cambridge, England

January 11: "Spiritual Elements of Social Service," Rev. Clarence R. Skinner

January 18: "Ethical Culture," Dr. Stanton Coit, Leader of Ethical Culture, London, England

January 25: "World Problem of the Colorline," Dr. W. E. B. Dubois, Director of the Association for the Advancement of Colored People[18]

In arranging the forum programs, Skinner doubtless remembered what a strong drawing card his uncle Otis had been
in Mt. Vernon and thus tried to schedule as many well-known
people as possible. Since his contacts were still limited, he was
forced to rely heavily on speakers' bureaus as a source; later in
Boston, after his reputation had become established, he had no
difficulty in extending the invitations himself.

Clarence Skinner later summarized the success of the Lowell
Forum in these words:

> A forum has been in operation at Grace Church, Lowell,
> Mass., for four years. Some of the most brilliant speak-
> ers of America and England have delivered messages
> from this platform, and the response in this community
> has been hardy, attendance averaging between two hun-
> dred and four hundred. Several effects have been noted.
> First, the attendance of the unchurched, especially men.
> Second, the attendance of men and women representa-
> tive of the various labor groups, such as unionists,
> socialists, etc. Third, the influence of these meetings
> beyond the narrow circle of those who attend. The press
> has been generous in reporting the speeches, and these
> speeches have been eagerly read by large numbers of
> the public. Fourth, it has placed the pulpit of Grace
> Church at the front as one of the recognized agencies of
> social advance in the community. Fifth, and to the mind
> of the writer, the most important of all, it has united the
> social question with religion in the minds of the people.
> The great need and demand of the age is for a spiritual
> interpretation of the whole of life. No other institution
> can do this more vigorously than the forum. Sixth, the
> immediate effect upon the church is beginning to be felt
> in the morning congregation. Many families, finding in
> the forum a satisfaction of their religious needs, have
> come to the regular services of the church. Seventh, the
> effect upon the other churches of the city is by no

means to be overlooked. It has stimulated their social service activities, and some churches in other sections of the city are using similar methods.[19]

That the church was undergoing substantial growth is evident from the record. By the end of 1914 there were some 260 families in its constituency; church school enrollment had risen to 220; and the Mission Circle's membership had increased from eighteen to fifty-six. Skinner was a conscientious pastor, and as his counseling load and parish calling increased, he developed the habit of working late at night. There were demands outside the church as well; he was elected president of the Massachusetts Sunday School Association, continued as secretary of the denominational Commission on Social Services, was appointed chair of the commission's youth committee, and delivered an address at a St. Lawrence commencement. It was a demanding life, but Clarence Skinner appears to have thrived on it. Meanwhile, his reputation within the denomination was growing rapidly.[20]

One of those invited to speak at the forum during the 1913-14 church year was Lee S. McCollester, dean of the Crane Theological School at Tufts College. The Skinners had invited McCollester to supper before the evening's program, and during the meal the dean had said to his host, "I'd like to have you come down to Tufts." Clarence didn't take the remark seriously, thinking such an idea beyond the realm of possibility, but not long afterward he received an offer to join the Crane faculty as professor of applied Christianity. Although he had been at Lowell for only three years, it did not take him long to decide; Clarence had found that he loved to teach, and the prospect of making it a career while still serving the church was too tempting to refuse. Thus in the fall of 1914, Clarence Skinner, a thirty-three-year-old with no theological degree and only eight years of parish experience, entered the academic world. His ministry at Lowell had proved a stepping-stone to greater things and Grace Church was proud of him. As his successor, Herbert Benton, later put it, "Skinner had a great success there. All the church was loud in praise."[21]

When Lee McCollester had come to the Crane Theological School in 1912, the school was at a low ebb, with only four full-time students. In fact, it was only through a concerted effort by Frederick Bisbee, editor of the *Universalist Leader*, to muster support for the school that it had been saved from being closed by the Tufts College administration. McCollester had finally been persuaded to accept the deanship after his demands were met for an adequate salary and the guarantee of a free hand in rebuilding the school's program; under his leadership the faculty was strengthened and the school began to show steady growth. One of his first appointments was that of Skinner. Herman C. Bumpus had just assumed the college presidency when Skinner arrived in the fall of 1914; at that time the student body numbered 479, with thirteen students in the theological school. The new professor was given a heavy teaching load from the start—in the first two years he was listed as teaching eighteen courses in applied Christianity, history of religions, church history, and religious education—not, of course, at the same time. In addition, he held the position of instructor in the Department of New Testament. Skinner lost no time in organizing the Department of Applied Christianity; by the 1916-17 school year, the department offered courses in social psychology, principles and methods of social service, home and foreign missions, country church problems, and laboratory social work, the latter requiring students to work in approved social agencies, settlement houses, or charitable organizations.[22]

Despite this seemingly overwhelming teaching and administrative load, Skinner also found time to write. In 1915 his first book, *The Social Implications of Universalism*, appeared; it was to have an immediate impact on the denomination. Its foreword began with the statement, "How to transform this old earth into the Kingdom of Heaven—that's the primal question," and the book went on to spell out the implications of Universalism for the Social Gospel in sweeping terms, going well beyond the scope of Protestant Christianity. Following the foreword were eleven short chapters, which, with little change, had also appeared in serial form in the *Universalist Leader*. The scope of Skinner's book is indicated by the titles of these chapters: "The Challenge," "A Free Church," "God and Democracy," "The Nature of Man," "Brotherhood," "Social Motive," "The Leadership of Jesus," "Hell and Salvation," "The New Unity," "The Final Triumph," and "The Larger Faith."

"The Challenge," Skinner asserted, is for Universalism to embody a religion relevant to contemporary life,

a religion which will be founded upon a twentieth century psychology and theology, a religion which is throbbing with the dynamics of democracy, a spirituality which expresses itself in terms of humanism, rather than in terms of individualism. . . . The traditional Protestant Church is dying. . . . The theology upon which it is built is dying; the individualism which called it into being is dying; the social order which it expressed is dying. Why should it not also die?[23]

It was time for a new church, a new theology, a new sense of interdependence, a new social order.

"A Free Church" must be an expression of free religion. The genius of Universalism is liberty. . . . Universalists are freemen. . . . If they are true to the spirit of their faith, they pledge themselves to free humanity from the economic degradation which fetters it, body, mind and soul, in this twentieth century. The logic is relentless, the implication clear. Universalism, by its very genius, is led into the great social maelstrom, because it is essentially a battle for the freedom of the common man.[24]

Skinner invoked the prophetic vision and spirit of historic Universalism. "Such will be the untrammeled spirit of the new religion, and by such motive will the new church be inspired."[25]

Skinner saw a close interrelationship between "God and Democracy."

As man attains increasing democracy, he conceives God as being more universal, more just and more intimately associated with life; and as God is conceived to be more just and intimate, the idea begets more democracy among men. Social action and theological reaction are equal, and in the same direction. . . . The Universalist idea of God is that of a universal, impartial, immanent spirit whose nature is love. It is the largest thought the world has ever known; it is the most revolutionary doctrine ever proclaimed; it is the most expansive hope ever dreamed. This is the God of modern man, and the God who is in modern man. . . . The Universal Fatherhood of God, which clearly implies democracy, does not imply equality, for equality does not appear in nature. . . . Democracy does not mean equality. It means the very opposite; its primary aim . . . is "the organization of society with respect to the individual."[26]

"The Nature of Man" is essentially God-like, he claimed, since humans are the children of God.

It is [the] thought of the preciousness and innate nobility of human nature which forms the distinctive characteristic of the great humanitarian movements of the nineteenth and twentieth centuries. . . . Let us trumpet abroad the transforming faith in man's innate worth and rouse society to its noblest endeavors by appeal to the divine nature. This is the ultimate incentive to the salvation of the world and to the beginning of the new social order. . . . The outstanding fact in this new social order would be the universal recognition of God the Father, and of all men as essentially spiritual beings. This theology of the divine indwelling . . . would transform prison systems and shops. It would work its revolution in mine and mill. It would seize upon wars, despotisms, slavery, and abolish them. It would beget itself in flesh and blood. It would be the most actual, astonishing and manifest fact in the world.[27]

"Faith in the transforming power of 'Brotherhood' is growing great," asserted Skinner.

The idea of Universal Brotherhood is the great social dynamic of the twentieth century. . . . And Universalism inspires this faith [in the spirit of brotherhood] not only because it teaches the divine origin of all men, but likewise because of its belief in the common destiny of humanity in all times and in all stations of life. . . . The new enthusiasm for humanity readily pictures a time when through eugenics, education, friendship, play, worship and work, the criminal will be no more, because the misdirection or the underdevelopment of human nature will cease.[28]

A new, forward-looking "Social Motive" is necessary for progress toward establishing the new order.

The true social objective is the perfecting of human character by the progressive improvement of those conditions and environments which are within the social control, and which largely determine character. It is obvious, therefore, that social work, in its larger and more radical meaning, arises out of two axiomatic assumptions . . . ; namely, that human character can be perfected, and that environmental conditions can be so spiritualized that they may be proper instruments for perfecting character. It is evident that the philosophy of Universalism implies social motive, since from its beginning it has interpreted all life as being essentially good, and the world as being capable of salvation. This belief is the true dynamic of social endeavor.[29]

"The Leadership of Jesus" was reaffirmed.

[T]he liberal faith stresses the achievement of salvation through the employment of the active and socially effective virtues of love, cooperation and brotherhood taught by Jesus and emphasized by Him as the true redemptive forces. . . . The attitude of Universalism toward Jesus is precisely that which the modern world is assuming in increasing geometric ratio; it is that which the social movement assumes. It is the attitude which develops the social motive, for the Universalist faith does not dogmatize about or define the person of Christ. Its shibboleth is the splendid statement in the articles of faith: "We believe in the spiritual authority and leadership of Jesus," a simple statement which is yet basic and comprehensive.[30]

Skinner, in his chapter on "Hell and Salvation," while rejecting the idea of eternal punishment, at the same time recognized a hell on earth.

Universalism has not abolished the idea of hell. *It has humanized and socialized it.* It has established human misery as the direct consequence of human action. The existence of such a hell can be demonstrated, the sting of its lash can be felt, the horror of it can be seen. The broken nerves of the *roué*, the rotting flesh of the prostitute, the moral degeneracy of the sensualist, the blood-red conscience of the murderer, are hell. There is no caprice in its operation, there is no trap door for escape. It is the most real, the most inevitable fact conceivable. To believe that every individual will suffer the just consequences of sin is the hardest, most disciplinary faith known. [This social hell is the result of] instituted customs and practices for which society is responsible, which can be eradicated out of the world. And Universalism has not only humanized and socialized hell, but it has humanized and socialized salvation. . . . [A] man must not only work out his own salvation; he must work out the salvation of the world. He is enmeshed in a world of humanity from which he can by no means wholly disentangle himself. He is part of the marvelous solidarity of life. He is shot through with psychic forces which he cannot escape. He is caught up in the mystic sway of standards and impulsions which grip him as the ocean grips a grain of sand. He cannot be saved except as he spiritualizes and Christianizes all the influences which are consciously or unconsciously molding character.[31]

Skinner made clear his conviction that the old ideas of hell and salvation were not only outmoded, they were dangerous and "anti-social, and must be perforce discarded before the new religion can gain the allegiance of the people."[32]

In "The New Unity" Skinner called on Universalists to take leadership in establishing a new unity of religious forces throughout the world.

The sectarian divisiveness of today is more than theologically deplorable, it is a social sin. . . . A new unity, more effective because more spontaneous and more democratic, must germinate through the long years of individualism. But it is coming. This unity has the inevitableness of destiny, for it is the unforced and unpreventable expression in terms of religion, of that larger unity which is sweeping through the world. Despite the high degree of diversity and specialization visible on the surface of life today, there is a more essential and patent unity underlying the modern world than has ever been known. . . . Religion feels and voices the new social solidarity. . . . Before such a consummation . . . is achieved two processes must be fulfilled. First, a growing out of the petty sectarian views of the past; and second, the normal growth of a larger, more inclusive faith. . . . Man's mind shall become more inclusive, his spirit more democratic, his intuitions more cosmic. . . . The new faith of the new unity of man will be the new Universalism.[33]

In "The Final Triumph" Skinner identified

the most distinctive contribution which Universalism has made to the development of theology and religion [as] the idea of the universal salvation of all souls and its concomitant of the final triumph of good over evil. . . . This triumphant hope in the ultimate salvation of humanity does not arise out of blindness to the hard facts of reality. . . . The vision of the Universalist is founded upon the marvelous discoveries and inventions which have taken place during the last century in the field of medicine, education, economics, industry and above all in social work. Gathering all the evidence from these sources, weighing it, and considering it in relation to the future of humanity, we learn that the hope which was instinctive and impulsive in the new religion rests upon the "reasoned optimism" of factual revelation.[34]

The prevention of diseases, crime, congenital defects, alcoholism, ignorance, inadequate housing, poverty, and war will be possible "when the conscience of men becomes sufficiently sensitized, socialized and energized."[35]

Universalists, Unitarians, and Quakers have started humanity on its the way to "The Larger Faith." This larger faith has already given

a larger outlook to men's intellectual conceptions of the universe; it [has] meant the deepening and enriching of spiritual experience by liberating ideas and emotions of infinite love; it [has] bound men together in a new unity of divine origins; it [has] dignified common humanity with the potentialities of the Christ life. . . . The great social passion of this age is essentially a movement toward the larger life. . . . Universalism and the social movement are thus of the same genius, as their ends are identical. The one contributes to the enlarging life by an expansive hope and a cosmic faith, the other by making available the resources of science, education and industry. . . . With such enlargement of the function of religion and with such enrichment of the personal life, Universalism is generically allied, for its whole passion is to bring the human soul into the realization of all its potentialities until it attains the stature of the perfect man. To that divinely human end, it unfolds before our vision the unities, the eternities and the universals, and bids us to live in conscious communion with them.[36]

To the present-day reader, Skinner's views in this book seem naive, his optimism unjustified. Moreover, he failed to address adequately some important questions, among them, the relationship of Christianity to the larger faith, the question of an afterlife, and the nature of individual salvation in the interim period before the final triumph. The book was, of course, written at a time when the proponents of the Social Gospel were filled with an optimism that was soon to be greatly tempered if not destroyed by subsequent events. Nevertheless, *The Social Implications of Universalism* represented a serious attempt to spell out a prophetic and comprehensive theological, ecclesiastical, and social program for the denomination, the first such effort in many years. As such, it made an immediate impact and established Clarence Skinner as one of Universalism's leading spokespersons.

Not long afterward, in May 1917, the Massachusetts Universalist Convention adopted a revised statement of faith prepared by Skinner and calling for a new commitment to social relevance. It read in part "the day of servitude for man is gone forever and the world sweeps forward to freedom and democracy. Wherever fetters are, they must fall; wherever exploitation holds sway, it must cease. Complete justice must secure universal opportunity for all men."[37] The statement found approval by the Ohio Convention as well; it passed a resolution "commending the new statement of Universalism prepared by Professor Skinner."[38]

That fall a Declaration of Social Principles was submitted to the Universalist General Convention by the Commission on Social Service. The declaration, adopted as the denomination's basis for social witness, clearly shows Skinner's influence as the commission's secretary. The preamble to the declaration's working program stated that, "through all the agencies of the church we shall endeavor to educate and inspire the community and the nation to a keener social consciousness and a truer vision of the kingdom of God on the earth." It went on to advocate the strengthening of marriage and the nurturing of children, a more equitable economic system, the rights of women, free and open discussion as "the soul of democracy," prohibition of the manufacture and sale of alcoholic beverages, the institution of "some form of social insurance," and formation of a world federation to secure peace. In conclusion, the declaration outlined a program for "completing humanity" that called for the following:

> *First:* An Economic Order which shall give to every human being an equal share in the common gifts of

God, and in addition all that he shall earn by his own labor.

Second: A Social Order in which there shall be equal rights for all, special privileges for none, the help of the strong for the weak until the weak become strong.

Third: A Moral Order in which all human law and action shall be an expression of the moral order of the universe.

Fourth: A Spiritual Order which shall build out of the growing lives of living men the growing temple of the living God.[39]

Further evidence of Skinner's emerging leadership was his appointment in 1918 as chair of the Massachusetts Convention's Commission on Social Welfare; a year later he was elected convention president. His philosophy was "that as far as possible we should preach a constructive program, making wherever possible recommendations rather than simply protesting and destroying." But there were occasions when protest was necessary. At all times "we must have a hatred of war, we must despise slavery, we must denounce exploitation."[40]

Despite his writing and denominational involvement, Skinner's primary commitment throughout these years was to his teaching and students at Crane. "I know of no way to accomplish [the restructuring of] the social order except through education," he had told the Sunday School Convention in 1917 and he put his major effort toward that end. He had developed three rules for successful teaching: first, a teacher must love to teach; second, a teacher must be an inspirer, not merely a transmitter of information and ideas; third, a teacher must always be a student. It was evident to those who knew him in the classroom that he qualified easily on the first of these requirements; the second he met not only from his teaching style, but also through his close personal contact with his students both at the school and at the Skinners' home; the third he met through continual reflection on his life experiences and through voluminous reading.[41]

Meanwhile, in 1917 the United States had entered World War I and Skinner's pacifism soon became a matter of controversy. He was one of only a handful of Universalist ministers to publicly declare a pacifist position. The overwhelming majority of his colleagues were active supporters of the war effort; so too were the administration and faculty of Tufts College. The facilities of the theological school were taken over by the military—Paige Hall by the Navy, Dean McCollester's office in Packard Hall by the Army. Those few students who remained in the school attended most of their classes in the dean's living room. After the Boston newspapers identified Skinner as a pacifist he was publicly ostracized, with President Bumpus so angry that he refused to recognize him when they met on campus. Most of the faculty, unable to change his mind even through prayer at faculty meetings, shunned him as well; there were calls for his dismissal. An atmosphere of near hysteria prevailed on campus; Bumpus had even provided wooden clubs for the students, so that they could repel enemy attacks on College Hill. Fortunately Skinner had several supporters in the faculty, including McCollester, who, although not a pacifist, defended his young professor's right to hold and express such views. Once, when Skinner was speaking in Concord, rotten eggs were thrown at him, but he never wavered, nor did he completely lose his sense of humor. In a letter to Bumpus in July 1917, he wrote,

> I hope that among the great cares you can find some relaxation and rest this summer, and that college matters will so shape themselves that you may be relieved of some of the great anxieties of the past. I doubt not that I have been one of these causes of worry.
>
> Sincerely, your pacifist friend,
> Clarence R. Skinner[42]

But despite this attempt at lightheartedness, the treatment he received during the war hurt Skinner deeply, and the wounds never completely healed.[43]

The end of the war brought a renewal of the nation's former optimism. As President Warren G. Harding put it, "America's present need is not heroics but healing, not nostrums but normalcy."[44] Skinner shared the optimism. In a piece written in January 1919 titled, "The World Soul," he waxed eloquently as he saw the dawning of new hope and the coming of a new day of peace and fulfillment throughout a united world: "Incarnation—Resurrection—Fulfillment. A World is born! 'Arise and shine, for *Thy* Light is come.'"[45] Clarence Skinner went out into the world to help speed the coming of the new day, but his optimism proved short-lived; the world was not ready for his message. Following an address in Meriden, Connecticut, in February 1919, the local newspaper quoted the city's mayor, Henry King, as saying he was "more than disgusted at the reported reference to Lenin in the so-called lecture. . . . We want no more of that stuff put out here and this may as well be known now as later, and trouble prevented."[46] Then, at the end of that year, Skinner's part-time ministry at the Medford Hillside Universalist Church, adjacent to the Tufts campus, was terminated. In addition to carrying on a successful church program for the previous two years, he had made the church a working laboratory, with his students participating in the church school and occasionally preaching. There had been mounting criticism, however, of his pacifism, and in the end he was forced to resign.

Further criticism of Skinner's views erupted at this time. He had delivered an address to the American Forum at Fanueil Hall on December 21 that had prompted complaints to the local district attorney, Nathan A. Tufts, who wrote to the Tufts administration asking for an investigation of Skinner. Fortunately for the latter, Bumpus had been replaced as college president by John Cousens, who replied to Tufts as follows:

> I have received some report of the meeting, from which it appears that after Professor Skinner's speech had been

delivered there was some little excitement and disturbance in connection with the speeches from the floor. I
fail to understand why a disturbance should have re-
sulted from anything which Professor Skinner said.

I have a very high regard for Professor Skinner per-
sonally as I know him to be a man of sincerity and
honesty of purpose.[47]

District Attorney Tufts answered promptly:

I have a letter before me from two persons who heard
his speech at Faneuil Hall, and they say that he approved the action taken by the I.W.W.s [members of the
International Workers of the World, a labor union out-
lawed in 1917] at Centralia when four soldiers were
shot during a parade; that he called the members of the
American Legion "anarchists"; that he spoke against the
measure introduced by Representative Johnson of Washington designed to curb undesirable immigration.[48]

President Cousens replied that he had read the speech and
did not interpret it that way, again reaffirming his confidence
in Skinner. The matter then appears to have been dropped.[49]
That same month Cousens received a letter from Arthur
Newhall, an alumnus, enclosing a clipping from a Lynn, Massachusetts, newspaper that referred to an address by Skinner at
the Congregational church on the subject of "Industrial Democracy." In it Skinner had called for improved working
conditions and the right to collective bargaining. "In view of
the present campaign to raise money for increasing salaries of
Tufts professors," wrote Newhall, "I should like to inquire if
this is the kind of 'stuff' which we are expected to support." It
was the second time in a few weeks that Skinner's views had
been referred to as "stuff." Cousens was understandably diplo-
matic in his reply. "I think you will recognize in the account
. . . ," he wrote, "some of the usual American newspaper

extravagance of statement," and he further suggested that allowances be made for an honest difference of opinion.[50]

Clarence Skinner's liberal views evoked suspicion not only in America, but in other lands as well. In 1922 he applied for a year's leave of absence to visit India under the auspices of those "interested in international and industrial peace," probably hoping to see Mohandas Gandhi, who by this time had been proclaimed by John Haynes Holmes as "the greatest man in the world." Skinner received permission from both Cousens and McCollester to make the trip, only to have his visa application turned down by the British government, which evidently feared that his visit would prove disruptive.[51]

Not surprisingly, Skinner became discouraged by the rejection of his views and the criticisms levelled against him, some from within his own denomination. The country was in a state of reaction to liberal idealism; membership in the League of Nations had been rejected; the Universalist denomination was experiencing an alarming decline; few of its churches seemed committed to implementing its social program; the Social Gospel movement was all but dead. Out of his deep disappointment, but still with ultimate hope, he wrote "In Times of Disillusion":

The world has grown unutterably old—
A place of bitter disillusionment.
Like some sad ruin out of ancient time
Half buried in obliterating sand,—
So seems the gallant world of yesteryear
To one who fellowshipped with wistful dreams.

Fair hopes did blossom for a flaming hour
And they were radiant. Bright youth went forth
In high imaginings, and all the world
Expectant and aglow, went forth with them
To greet the new age and new inbrothering.

But now the heart of the world is broken and sad,
The dream is spent—the curtains drawn—and those
Who strode to martial music, spoke great words
Befitting those great days, have laid aside
The mask of Jove-like visage and have shrunk
To lesser mould to play the cynic's part.
The candle that so mightily illumined
Has sputtered and gone out.
The house where we held rendezvous with hope
Is dark. The dream is gone. The dreamers go
In sad dismay to disillusionment.

Does God change masks when the curtain's drawn,
Put off high resolution and descend
To lower levels to play a lesser part?
Not God! That cannot be. No, God's not through.
There's hope immense to keep hope strong
And thrill the dreamer's soul with battle-call.
God's unsurrendered! He's God in that.
God's unsurrendered! So am I! For dreams
Outlast the dreamer. And when the great event
Is chronicled, 'tis vision will prove true—
The final truth in all events—supreme and ultimate.

Therefore I'll dream.
I'll light the candle yet again, illumine
The dark forsaken house, bring back the folk
Who thrilled at glimpses of a fairer world,
People the stage with pageantry and bid
Full panoplied illusion still enact
The epic of inbrothering.
I'll summon from out of time's unfathomed store
Great souls who, in the midst of hopeless days
Kept faith and knew the loneliness of God.
Those splendid deaths and yet more splendid lives
Which rallied their faltering age with valiantness

And left strong memories to breed strong hopes.
For such undying fellowship has power
To swell our shrunken souls to ampler mould,
And make us truer men.

I'll still proclaim the "Vision Splendid,"
'Till it strikes God-fire
In old and broken hearts, and urges on
The world to consummate its dream.
God's unsurrendered! SO AM I! Therefore
I will live communicate with hope. I light
The candle and—I DREAM.[52]

This piece represented Clarence Skinner at his poetic best and gives insight into the prophetic vision that was central to his being, that of the transformation of "this old earth into the Kingdom of Heaven." The transformation might take longer than he had previously thought, but that it would someday be accomplished, he remained confident. In the meantime, he would do all he could to help that transformation along and to keep that vision alive. In a time when many surrendered, he was, indeed, unsurrendered.[53]

Fortunately Skinner was soon to find a vehicle that would help lift him out of disillusionment and disappointment. His commitment to the church as an institution essential for the transformation had remained unshaken and in the fall of 1919, while he was being forced out of his ministry to the Hillside congregation, he conceived a plan for a radically new kind of church, one which would be all-inclusive, unrestrained by denominational ties. It marked his disengagement from the mainstream of the Universalist denomination, which would continue for the next fifteen years. Ever conscientious, Skinner took pains to keep President Cousens informed as to what he was doing; the latter asked only that nothing be done that would prove embarrassing to Dean McCollester.[54]

In October an announcement was circulated advertising a

meeting to discuss the possible organization of a community church in Boston. John Haynes Holmes, who had just severed his Unitarian ties and led the transformation of the Unitarian Church of the Messiah into the independent Community Church of New York, was present; he and Skinner had been drawn together by their theological and social liberalism, their pacifism, and their desire to create a model for a more relevant church. Attendance at the meeting was small, but there appeared to be enough interest in the proposal to proceed. Accordingly, a series of experimental services was initiated, with Holmes scheduled as the first speaker. On January 11 a congregation of three hundred assembled in Steinert Hall to hear his address on "The Character and Meaning of the Community Church Movement." Skinner himself preached on the following Sunday, followed by such notables as Bishop Paul Jones, Norman Thomas, and Frank Oliver Hall. Undoubtedly Skinner's experience with the Lowell Forum played a part in the planning. Attendance during those early services ranged from sixty to five hundred, with Holmes attracting the largest congregations.[55]

On the basis of this encouraging start, an organizational meeting of "The Community Church of Boston" was held on October 31, 1920, following the Sunday service; officers were elected, including Skinner as chair. A statement of purpose was adopted that, after revision and approval by the church's constituency, read as follows:

> The Community Church of Boston is a free fellowship of men and women united for the study of universal religion, seeking to apply ethical ideals to individual life and the co-operative principle to all forms of social and economic life.

The only condition for membership was subscription to the following Bond of Union:

We, the undersigned, accepting the stated Purpose of this Church, so join ourselves together that we may help one another, may multiply the power of each through mutual fellowship, and thereby promote most effectively the cause of truth, righteousness and love in the world.[56]

For the next fifteen years Clarence Skinner was to fill what were essentially two full-time jobs—faculty member at Crane Theological School and "leader" of the Community Church of Boston (the traditional term "minister" was not used). As leader he did much of the church's administrative and pastoral work, attended all meetings, planned and led the Sunday services, presided over rites of passage, and preached some three times a year. After the church became established, he was voted a modest salary, which helped offset some personal expenses. The services reflected the "rational worship" to which the congregation was committed and were simple in format—an invocation stating the church's purpose and creating an atmosphere of worship, three hymns (often with new words), a reading, a nonpetitionary prayer, and the sermon. A forum, consisting of comments, discussion, questions, and answers, followed each service. Holmes preached monthly, asking only that his expenses be covered; Skinner and John Randall preached at least three times a year. The other speakers, chosen carefully, included such well-known men and women as Rabbi Stephen S. Wise, Bertrand Russell, H. V. Kaltenborn, Maude Royden, Will Durant, Reinhold Niebuhr, Sarujini Naidu, Sherwood Eddy, William Ernest Hocking, Kirtley Mather, John Dietrich, and Margaret Sanger.

Services were held in rented halls throughout the period of Skinner's leadership, with the average attendance rising from 175 in 1921 to about 1,200 by 1926. The church's involvement in the Sacco and Vanzetti case in which two Italian immigrants were charged with murder and eventually executed (Clarence and Clara attended many sessions of the trial), the Scottsboro case in which nine black youths were unjustly charged with raping two white women, aid to the Republican government of Spain in its struggle against Fascism, and the right of birth control advocate Margaret Sanger to speak in Boston were perhaps the most publicized examples of its social concern.[57] It has been said that, for Skinner, his involvement in the Community Church was "a thrilling experience." As Charles Gaines has described it:

> The constant telephone calls from people who were supporting some cause, or even supporting no cause; the interesting people who spoke and listened each Sunday; the vital give and take in the Forum which probably brought back many memories of his college debating days. In all these instances, Clarence felt his greatest expression and challenge. After each Sunday he was at his highest point of emotion. The crowds moved him deeply and he always sparkled.[58]

He had, indeed, remained unsurrendered.

(A fuller treatment of Skinner's involvement in the Community Church of Boston is given in Carl Seaburg's "Clarence Skinner: Building a New Kind of Church," in this volume.)

Meanwhile, the Crane Theological School was undergoing a recovery after the end of the war. Skinner was organizing the Department of Applied Christianity into one of the best of its kind. Particularly popular was his course in social ethics, "a study of the great ethical concepts of Jesus as applied to modern society," in which various reform movements were studied with an effort to construct a picture of what a Christianized society would look like. Another popular course dealing directly with social work consisted of one lecture or conference per week, with the rest of students' time spent in field work with approved Boston agencies. "This experience in the laboratory of humanity," the catalog read, "is of inestimable value to all who are to deal with problems of leadership in industry, schools, communities and churches."

With the student body growing, Skinner's heavy teaching load was lightened somewhat by the addition to the school's faculty of J. A. C. Fagginer Auer in 1924 as professor of church history and philosophy of religion and John Ratcliff in 1927 as professor of religious education. Skinner's old mentor, Frank Oliver Hall, had joined the faculty in 1919 as professor of homiletics and continued in that position for ten years; he was replaced by Alfred S. Cole. Bruce Brotherston was appointed in 1930 to teach philosophy both in the school and in the college. McCollester himself served not only as dean, but also as professor of religious literature and college chaplain.[59]

In 1929 Skinner was appointed vice dean to relieve the aging McCollester from some of his duties. Teaching, however, remained Skinner's top priority; his willingness to express his own convictions in the classroom, while stimulating to all and inspiring to many, on occasion proved disturbing. During Skinner's criticism of the verdict in the Sacco-Vanzetti case, one student, Cornelius Greenway, became so angry that he walked out of the classroom.

> I dodged the classes for several weeks [he wrote] and everytime I saw Dr. Skinner, I made it my business to dodge him. He knew I was dodging him but he let me out like a deep-sea fisherman will let out his line and, by so doing, tire out what is at the end of the line. One day I saw him coming, made a quick about face and went on the other side of the college chapel, and that was just what he expected me to do, for in a manner of a minute or two we stood face to face; he with love and understanding in his heart and I with disgust and re-sentment and disapproval.[60]

In reaction to Skinner's views, another student, J. Vernon Muir, left school and abandoned his plans to enter the ministry.

> He seemed to have very fixed opinions [Muir wrote]
> and his teaching seemed socialistic or even communis-
> tic to us conservative Republicans. . . . As a trinitarian
> Congregationalist, I was confused and left my plans for
> the ministry.[61]

In the meantime, Skinner, in addition to teaching duties
and responsibilities with the Community Church, was continuing to write extensively. From 1921 to 1932, fifty-six
articles appeared under his name, several of them long enough
to appear in serial form. Whereas his earlier articles had
appeared for the most part in the denominational periodical
the *Universalist Leader* (renamed the *Christian Leader* in 1926),
during this period the vast majority were published in *Unity*, a
historically Unitarian periodical of which Holmes was editor,
with Skinner eventually becoming a contributing editor. Perhaps this change was prompted by his sense of alienation from
his own denomination; more probably the shift was a result of
his expanding religious horizons, evidenced by his involvement with the Community Church. At any rate, unlike John
Haynes Holmes, he retained his denominational connection.[62]
The humanist-theist debate was at its height during this period; while Skinner warmly welcomed humanists to the Community Church's pulpit, he felt strongly that the church should
not restrict itself by embracing humanism as its guiding philosophy. "The genius of the two movements is essentially
different," he contended, "and, therefore, each should develop
its own special history. . . . Any church that is as broad as the
community must surely be glad to enfold humanism, and any
true humanism . . . must be willing to co-operate with a
church which takes the whole community as its field, and the
help of all people as its high goal. But the two movements
must still go their divergent ways."[63]

On October 27, 1932, McCollester, by then seventy-three,
resigned from the deanship of the school, the name of which
had been expanded in 1925 to Tufts School of Religion, Crane

Theological School, to reflect its closer connection with the college and attract a broader student body. The school had grown significantly during McCollester's twenty-year tenure; the physical plant had been expanded and improved, and the student body had grown from four to forty-five including a number of Unitarians and other non-Universalists. In his letter of resignation McCollester had written, "It is of course not for me to dictate as to my successor, but it is proper for me to express to you the wish that the new Dean shall be Dr. Skinner." The trustees agreed; Skinner took over his new duties at once and was officially installed at a college worship service the following February. Even before his installation he had made it clear that changes could be expected under his leadership. In addressing the Universalist ministers of the Boston area on "The Universalist Church Twenty-five Years Hence," he predicted (accurately) that the denomination would become divided into conservative and progressive wings, and that he would be promoting the latter.[64]

Taking up his new responsibilities with characteristic enthusiasm, Skinner created a dean's fund as a source of loans to needy students, arranged for the installation of a kitchenette in Paige Hall for student use, served as a father figure for his students, and protected them from criticism. Soon after assuming the deanship, he and Clara moved from Cambridge to a home on the Tufts campus to be nearer the students and his work.

Despite his new administrative responsibilities, Skinner remained first of all a master teacher who continued to command his students' respect by his careful preparation, in-depth knowledge, communication skills, and concern for them as individuals. There was, however, a certain stand-offishness about him, undoubtedly stemming from his shyness; whereas students might have referred to his predecessor as "Mac," to them he was always "Dean Skinner" or "Dr. Skinner."[65] Former students have recalled how this shyness often made his contacts with them outside the classroom awkward, as when, out of a sense of responsibility as dean, he visited them in their dormitory rooms or when he and Clara had them to their home for dinner; conversations were strained as he tried hard to be sociable and friendly.

In the classroom, however, he was a different person— stimulating, confident, engaged,[66] his teaching regularly enlivened by spontaneous wit. Once when lecturing on comparative religions he stated that, "in every religion there is a trinity." Pausing a moment, he turned to one of his students and asked, "What is the trinity of Universalism?" When the student replied he didn't know, Skinner retorted, "Well, there isn't any!" On another occasion a student wrote on an exam paper, "Nirvana means nothing to me." Skinner gave him full credit for his answer and commented, "I am glad you have reached that state." Usually, in addition to his administrative responsibilities as dean, he taught two courses each semester; his courses in comparative religions and social ethics appear to have been especially popular.[67]

Meanwhile, Skinner's theological views, once considered radical, had gained wide acceptance within the denomination even if many of his social views had not. The Washington Avowal of Faith, adopted unanimously by the Universalist General Convention in 1935, clearly reflected his theology by avowing "faith in God and Eternal and All-Conquering Love, in the spiritual leadership of Jesus, in the supreme worth of every human personality, in the authority of truth known or to be known, and in the power of men of good-will and sacrificial spirit to overcome all evil and progressively establish the kingdom of God."[68]

In 1936, Skinner resigned from his position as leader of the Community Church of Boston. His increased responsibilities at Crane were undoubtedly a factor, but he also felt that after fifteen years the church would profit by new, full-time leadership. He was succeeded by Donald Lothrop, who served until 1974. Unlike the Mt. Vernon church, which did not long survive after Skinner's successful ministry, the Community

Church continues to this day, albeit in altered form, as a member of the Unitarian Universalist Association. John Haynes Holmes, reflecting on his "thirty years and more" of "work and happiness" with the church, recalled that

> [i]n storms of bitterness more terrible in World War II than any hurricane of wrath known as World War I, with the government engaged in the noisome business of making war upon its own citizens, this Boston church stood like a lighthouse at black midnight, shedding afar its saving light to guide good ships.[69]

With his promotion to the deanship and resignation from church leadership, Clarence Skinner entered a new phase of life. Thereafter he contributed almost exclusively as an educator—through his classroom teaching, many speaking engagements, and extensive writings. During the next decade he was author of four books plus some sixty articles, most of the latter published in the denominational periodical (by then renamed the *Christian Leader*) rather than in *Unity*, signalling his return to Universalism's mainstream. Particularly noteworthy was his Phi Beta Kappa address delivered at Tufts in 1934; entitled "This Revolutionary Age," it called on scholars to recognize and address the social revolution going on all around them. Certainly his credentials for giving such an address had been firmly established in academic circles; he had been awarded honorary doctorates from Meadville Theological School in 1926 and from St. Lawrence University in 1933, and was considered for the presidency of St. Lawrence before he withdrew his name.

In addition to his work as an educator, Skinner participated in other activities; he served as a board member of the American Civil Liberties Union and the League for Democratic Control and from 1935 until 1944 as secretary of the denomination's Social Welfare Commission. The latter work was discouraging, for times had changed and interest in social concerns was at a low ebb with little funding available.[70]

In 1937 Skinner's second book, *Liberalism Faces the Future*, was published (it had been two decades since *The Social Implications of Universalism* appeared). In it he defined liberalism as "the system that opposed illiberalism" rather than a body of knowledge, claiming it to be undefinable in static terms. "It can never be inherited, but must always be won by a new battle for each generation."[71] Two years later *Human Nature and the Nature of Evil* appeared, in which he first reviewed the approaches to the problem proposed by Barthianism (the Bible-based theological system of Karl Barth), nihilism, Christian Science, Freudianism, and environmentalism, all of which he found wanting. He addressed the subject from the standpoint of liberalism, claiming that although evil appears to be "an integral part of the normal man," the liberal also recognizes humanity's good nature and finds evil a stimulus to search for what is better. On the other hand, it is abnormal for good to produce evil. "There are not many," he wrote, "who would want sickness because they are well." There is in life a creative power that works toward unity; progress toward this unity is the answer to evil.[72] In both these books, Skinner's old concern for social improvement comes through clearly.

Also in 1939, a revised edition of *The Social Implications of Universalism* was published, reflecting the changes in Skinner's thinking that had occurred over the years; his Universalism is less tied to Christianity, and he is more realistic concerning the difficulties and time requirements for effecting social change.[73] *Hell's Ramparts Fell*, published in 1941, was in a completely different genre. A biography of John Murray co-authored with Alfred Cole, it was written to mark the bicentennial of Murray's birth. Cole did most of the research for the book, with Skinner writing chapters 2, 3, 4, 9, and 11. One has the sense that Skinner participated because of his close friendship with Cole and because he felt that, given the occasion, the book needed to be written.[74]

Meanwhile, Crane Theological School had grown steadily under Skinner's leadership as dean. By 1938 there were fifty-four students and a faculty of thirteen, most part time, but with a broad range of talents and interests. The composition of the student body was also varied, it being "an article of faith" with Skinner to make the school as inclusive as possible; Universalists, Unitarians, Congregationalists, Episcopalians, and Greek Orthodox of diverse backgrounds and varying abilities were part of the mix.[75]

In 1938 Skinner took his only sabbatical; he and Clara traveled across the continent, coming back through the Panama Canal. Typically, he stayed busy during the journey, filling numerous speaking engagements in Universalist and Unitarian circles along the way. On his return he pronounced himself "almost rested."[76]

The years during the Second World War were difficult for Skinner. He had entered his sixties; his energy was beginning to ebb; and there was no opportunity for vacations. While his pacifism did not become a subject of controversy, he must have derived satisfaction from the strong antiwar stands taken by the Community Church. When one of his students, Eugene Adams, was under fire for participating in an antiwar demonstration, Skinner called him into his office. "Gene, what's this I've been reading in the newspapers?" he asked, doubtless thinking of his own experience twenty-five years earlier. "Dean Skinner, I'm scared as hell," was the reply. Skinner chuckled. It was only natural to feel that way, given the situation, he said, adding, "Gene, if you feel all right inside for what you have done, you should have no fears."[77]

In 1945, as the war was ending, Clarence Skinner retired. He was only sixty-four, but he had undergone major surgery during the academic year for cancer of the rectum and he felt too tired to continue. Tufts honored him at commencement with a Doctor of Divinity, his third honorary degree.[78] Despite his ill health, he completed another book, *A Religion for Greatness*, published that year. It was dedicated to his old friend,

Louis Pink, who had made significant contributions through his work in public health, housing, and insurance. The book revealed how Skinner's thinking evolved over the years; it was to exert a significant influence in directing Universalism beyond the limits of Christianity and toward a universal religion.

Skinner had always had a mystical bent, but in *A Religion for Greatness* it had become full blown, with his practical social emphasis enriched by a deep-seated mysticism. He called for men and women to go deeper and recognize that there exists a radical religion that underlies all things and is indeed *the great reality*.[79]

> What, then, is this radical religion which goes down below surface appearance, and finds its root in the profoundest reality? . . . To sum the answer in a word, radical religion creates in man a sense of vital, meaningful relationship between self and the universe. . . . Groping through fogs of ignorance [humanity] laid hold on the central fact of human existence; namely, that there is a relationship between man and the powers which exist outside and beyond himself. . . . [There] stands out one impressive fact—namely, man touches infinity; his home is in immensity; he lives, moves, and has his being in eternity. This magnificent assertion is man's greatest affirmation.[80]

Skinner went on to discuss how a recognition of this radical religion could be applied to economics, race, politics, society, and science. If applied to economics, for example, the world would no longer tolerate a difference between wealth and poverty, surplus and starvation.

> The *agape* of the early Christians with its warm personal intimacy will be supplanted by something more formal and organized. Perhaps it will be implemented by governments, and be run as insurance, city plan-

ning, compulsory health measures, etc. Perhaps it will retain certain qualities of the voluntary system, as in our cooperative societies. Whatever it shall be, it must adopt the principles of responsibility for all men's welfare.[81]

Skinner was confident that out of the evolutionary process men and women would come to a deep, mystical understanding of their place in the universe and thus be inspired to live together in a new way, moving toward "the unities and the universals." "The religion of greatness looks to the day," he wrote in conclusion, "when truth, goodness and beauty will become indivisible parts of the all-embracing unity and universal."[82] The kingdom of heaven on earth might not be at hand, and Clarence Skinner would not live to see it, but he had faith that it would come, nevertheless. The prophet of a new Universalism was to remain unsurrendered to the end.

Clarence Skinner was a prolific and earnest writer, unafraid to address the pressing theological and social problems of his times. His writings, influential in their day, are important to the contemporary reader chiefly for the insight they give into the issues confronting Universalism and the theological and social contexts in which he lived. However, it is as an inspiring teacher, rather than as a writer, a social activist, or an ecclesiastical reformer that Skinner is best remembered.[83] In retirement he must have derived satisfaction from the efforts of the *Humiliati*, a group of his former students, as they worked to "universalize" Universalism along the general lines that he had come to advocate, and from the selection of fellow liberal and pacifist Clinton Lee Scott as superintendent of the powerful Massachusetts Universalist Convention, an appointment that he had helped to promote.[84]

The Skinners had looked forward to the time when Clarence retired and they would be able to enjoy travel and leisure together. They had already gone to Europe nine times over the years (their families were well-to-do and money was never a problem) and had visited every country on the continent, but there was still much more of the world to see. Unfortunately, their plans were greatly modified by Clarence's illness, with their trips shorter and carefully spaced. Several times he was confined to bed, often working on manuscripts while lying down. It is likely that the three manuscripts that were published posthumously as *Worship and a Well Ordered Life* were prepared at this time.[85]

Not long after his retirement, an oil portrait of Skinner was commissioned by the Crane Theological School alumni, to be hung in Crane Chapel with those of his predecessors as dean. The sittings, which were held in the studio of the artist, Joseph B. Cahill, in Portland, Maine, proved extremely tiring for Clarence, as did the necessary travel, but the project was successfully completed. The portrait was unveiled in December 1948 with hundreds on hand for the ceremony. John Haynes Holmes, his friend from the Community Church experiment, was the principal speaker for the occasion.[86]

Meanwhile the cancer had continued to spread, and by the spring of 1948 Skinner was told that it had entered his bloodstream. He was deeply disturbed by the report, reacting with uncharacteristic emotion, and spent several days preparing instructions for the disposition of his most important possessions. Among his requests were that his extensive collection of religious artifacts, accumulated during his travels, should go to the Crane Theological School and his books to the General Theological Library. The task had a calming effect; after it was completed, he resumed work on his manuscripts.[87]

By the summer of 1949 Skinner's condition was extremely grave. He and Clara were at their summer home in Long Ridge, Connecticut, where Louis Pink and Alfred Cole, two of his closest friends, visited, sensing the end was near. Pink urged that he be taken to the hospital, but Skinner refused. Nevertheless, Clara ordered an ambulance, hoping that he would change his mind when it arrived. He did not. When he saw the two attendants, he looked at Clara and said, "You know that I don't want to go to the hospital." The men were sent away; Clarence had stubbornly won. Within a week, on August 27, Clarence Skinner died at the age of sixty-eight. Funeral arrangements were placed in Cole's hands with the funeral held in Stamford three days later. Cole, Pink, John Ratcliff, Cornelius Greenway, and Roger Etz participated in the service with internment at the cemetery in Long Ridge, not far from where the couple had spent many summer vacations. Later, memorial services were held at Tufts and at the Community Church of Boston.[88]

A decade after his death, the Clarence R. Skinner Award was established, to be given annually for the sermon "best expressing Universalism's social principles." During the 1960s the *Annual Journal of the Universalist Historical Society* devoted considerable space to Skinner's contributions, including a re-printing of the 1915 edition of *The Social Implications of Universalism*.[89] Later, a newly acquired building at the denominational headquarters in Boston was named Skinner House, and Skinner House Books became the imprint for denominational publications primarily for a Unitarian Universalist readership.

Many tributes were paid to Clarence Skinner after his death, among them the following resolution, written on behalf of the Tufts faculty by Cole and Ratcliff, his successor as dean:

> The members of the Faculty of Arts and Sciences of Tufts College desire to express their deep sense of loss at the death of Clarence Russell Skinner at Stamford, Conn., August 27, 1949. Dr. Skinner joined our faculty in 1914 as Professor of Applied Christianity; in 1933 he became Dean of the School of Religion, retiring in 1945 after thirty-one years of service.
>
> From the many relationships and associations with Dean Skinner, which will long be remembered by faculty and students, we can record only a few ways in which he enriched and stimulated the life of our college community.

We would especially recall:

His love for his fellow men and his constant defense of human rights and civil liberties.

His untiring effort to erase racial and class barriers.

His uncompromising support of principles he felt to be right, in the face of severe criticism and hostility.

His outstanding ability as a preacher and lecturer.

His classroom teaching and its stimulating effect on the minds of his students.

His home on Sawyer Avenue, where Mrs. Skinner and he were generous in their hospitality to students, faculty, and guests at the college.

His ability as a writer to make clear and concise the great issues of liberal religion.

His untiring efforts in the cause of peace and understanding between the nations of the world.

His great interest in the universals and unities of life calling for a religion of greatness which would transcend all creeds.

His leadership in founding the Community Church of Boston and his far-reaching influence in other liberal institutions throughout the nation.

If to these notations could be added the personal tribute of each member of the faculty, it still would be only a small indication of the outstanding service of Dean Skinner to Tufts College, and but a small measure of the sense of indebtedness of the faculty for his life and work among us.[90]

Notes

1. Charles A. Gaines, "Clarence R. Skinner: Image of a Movement," unpublished BD thesis, Crane Theological School, 1961 (hereinafter referred to as Gaines), pp. 15-21 (based on "Charles M. Skinner: A Sketch of His Life and Tribute to His Work,"

Brooklyn Daily Eagle, 1908, pp. 3-14, 18; interview with Clara A. Skinner, July 1960, Cambridge, Massachusetts).

2. Gaines, pp. 22-24 (based on Alfred S. Cole, "A Short History of Tufts College School of Religion," Universalist Historical Society, June 1947, pp. 48-49).

3. Gaines, pp. 15-16, 22-23 (based on Louis H. Pink *et al. Candle in the Wilderness* (New York: Appleton-Century-Crofts, 1957), pp. 90-92; Richard Eddy, *Universalism in America: A History* (Boston: Universalist Publishing House, 1894), Vol. II, pp. 131-132, 416, 453, 465).

4. Gaines, pp. 24-26 (based on interview with Clara A. Skinner [hereinafter C. A. S.]).

5. Gaines, pp. 25, 28 (based on interview with C. A. S.).

6. Gaines, pp. 25, 26 (based on interview with C. A. S.).

7. Gaines, pp. 30-32 (based on interview with C. A. S.).

8. Gaines, pp. 30-33 (based on interview with C. A. S.; and *Universalist Yearbook* [Boston: Universalist Publishing House, 1906]).

9. *Universalist Leader*, March 19, 1910, p. 377 (cited in Gaines, pp. 35-36).

10. Gaines, p. 33 (based on interview with C. A. S.).

11. Gaines, pp. 34-35 (based on interview with C. A. S.).

12. *Universalist Leader*, March 26, 1910, p. 401; April 29, 1911, pp. 526-528; Alfred Cole, op. cit., pp. 49-50 (cited in Gaines, p. 37).

13. Gaines, pp. 29, 31, 36-38 (based on interview with C. A. S.; Louis Pink, "God's Unsurrendered," *Christian Leader*, October 1949, p. 352; Emerson Hugh Lalone, *And Thy Neighbor as Thyself* [Boston: Universalist Publishing House, 1959], pp. 68-75; *Universalist Yearbook*, 1909).

14. Gaines, pp. 38-39 (based on interview with C. A. S.).

15. Gaines, p. 40 (based on *Universalist Yearbook*, 1912); *Universalist Leader*, October 14, 1911, p. 1037 (cited in Gaines, p. 41).

16. Skinner, *Survey*, January 13, 1912, quoted in James Hunt, "Clarence R. Skinner and the Social Gospel Movement," unpublished manuscript, May 3, 1956 (cited by Gaines, p. 43).

17. *Universalist Leader*, May 19, 1917, p. 316 (cited by Gaines, p. 44).

18. Gaines, p. 45; *Universalist Leader*, January 10, 1914 (cited by Gaines, p. 46).

19. *Universalist Leader*, February 13, 1915 (cited by Gaines, p. 47-48).
20. Gaines, pp. 42-43 (based on *Universalist Yearbooks*, 1913, 1914; interview with C. A. S.; and *Universalist Leader*, June 7, 1913, p. 718).
21. Gaines, pp. 48-49 (based on interview with C. A. S.); letter, Herbert E. Benton to Gaines, October 17, 1960 (cited by Gaines, p. 49).
22. Gaines, pp. 50-52 (based on Cole, op. cit., pp. 34-40; John M. Ratcliff, address, Skinner portrait unveiling ceremony, December 6, 1948).
23. Skinner, *The Social Implications of Universalism*, reprinted in the *Journal of the Universalist Historical Society*, Volume V, 1964-65, pp. 91, 90.
24. Ibid., pp. 93-94.
25. Ibid., p. 95.
26. Ibid., pp. 95-96, 98.
27. Ibid., pp. 100-101.
28. Ibid., pp. 102-104.
29. Ibid., pp. 107-108.
30. Ibid., pp. 110-111.
31. Ibid., pp. 112-113.
32. Ibid., p. 113.
33. Ibid., pp. 114-117.
34. Ibid., pp. 117-118.
35. Ibid., pp. 117-118.
36. Ibid., pp. 120-122.
37. *Yearbook*, Massachusetts Universalist Convention, 1917 (cited in Gaines, p. 56); *Universalist Leader*, June 9, 1917, p. 369.
38. Lalone, op. cit., p. 76 (cited in Gaines, pp. 56-57).
39. Ibid., Appendix (cited in Gaines, p. 57).
40. Gaines, pp. 57-58 (based on *Yearbooks*, Massachusetts Universalist Convention, 1917, 1918, 1919); *Christian Leader*, June 3, 1933 (cited by Gaines, p. 40).
41. Gaines, pp. 58-59 (based on *Universalist Leader*, July 28, 1917, p. 491; *Unity*, November 5, 1928).
42. Letter, Skinner to Hermon C. Bumpus, July 14, 1917, Tufts University Archives (cited in Gaines, p. 68).
43. Gaines, p. 68 (based on interview with Donald Lothrop).

44. John Hicks, *The American Nation* (Cambridge, Massachusetts: Houghton Mifflin, 1955), p. 455 (cited in Gaines, p. 69).

45. *Universalist Leader*, January 11, 1919, p. 40 (cited in Gaines, pp. 70-71).

46. Gaines, pp. 71-72 (based on *Morning Record*, Meriden, Connecticut, February 14, 1919, Tufts University Archives; interview with Donald Sleeper, March 1, 1961, Medford, Massachusetts; *Universalist Leader*, December 1, 1918, p. 864).

47. Letter, John Cousens to Nathan Tufts, January 3, 1920, Tufts University Archives (cited in Gaines, p. 73).

48. Letter, Nathan Tufts to John Cousens, January 6, 1920, Tufts University Archives (cited in Gaines, p. 73).

49. Gaines, p. 72.

50. Letter, Arthur Newhall to John Cousens, January 15, 1920, with article, Tufts University Archives; letter, John Cousens to Arthur Newhall, January 20, 1920, Tufts University Archives (cited in Gaines, p. 74).

51. Gaines, pp. 74-75 (based in part on letter, Skinner to John Cousens, July 19, 1922, Tufts University Archives).

52. *Unity*, April 24, 1924, p. 119 (cited in Gaines, pp. 75-76). (See also, Gaines, "Clarence R. Skinner: The Dark Years," *Annual Journal of the Universalist Historical Society*, Vol. III, 1962, pp. 1-13, for an account of this period [1917-1924] in Skinner's life, an edited version of pp. 61-78 of Gaines's BD thesis.)

53. Gaines, pp. 75-77.

54. Gaines, p. 81 (based on letter, John Cousens's secretary to Skinner, October 22, 1919, Tufts University Archives).

55. Gaines, p. 81 (based on "The Community Church of Boston: History and Principles," 1939, pp. 4-5; Skinner, Ed., *A Free Pulpit in Action* [New York: Macmillan, 1931], p.1).

56. "The Community Church of Boston," p. 22 (cited in Gaines, p. 82).

57. Gaines, pp. 82-92 (based on interviews with Lothrop and C. A. S.; yearly reports and church records, Community Church of Boston; Hunt, op. cit.; Skinner, Ed., *A Free Pulpit in Action*, pp. 1-17).

58. Gaines, p. 89.

59. Gaines, pp. 52-53 (based on Ratcliff address, cited in footnote 22); *Catalogue of Tufts College*, 1928-29, pp. 164-171.

60. Letter, Cornelius Greenway to Charles Gaines, June 30, 1960 (cited in Gaines, p. 54).
61. Letter, J. Vernon Muir to Charles Gaines, July 7, 1960 (cited in Gaines, p. 54).
62. Alan Seaburg, "The Writings of Dean Skinner: A Bibliography," *Annual Journal of the Universalist Historical Society*, Volume V, 1964-65, pp. 65-67.
63. Skinner, "Humanism and the Community Church," *Christian Leader*, May 17, 1930, pp. 625-626 (reprinted from *Unity*).
64. Gaines, pp. 110-111 (based in part on Cole, op. cit., p. 28); *Christian Leader*, January 21, 1933, pp. 66, 93-94.
65. Gaines, pp. 112-117 (based on interviews with C. A. S. and Frederick L. Harrison, July 1960; letter, John Cousens to Skinner, December 12, 1933, Tufts University Archives; letter, Stanley F. Murray to Gaines, August 5, 1960; letter, Albert Perry to Gaines, August 5, 1960; letter, Eric Alton Ayer to Gaines, July 12, 1960).
66. Charles A. Howe, interviews with Gordon McKeeman and Carl Seaburg, February 1-2, 1993.
67. Gaines, p. 114 (based on interview with Harrison; letter, Horace Westwood to Charles Gaines, September 9, 1960); Howe interview with McKeeman.
68. Russell E. Miller, *The Larger Hope* (Boston: Unitarian Universalist Association, 1985), pp. 114-115.
69. John Haynes Holmes, *I Speak for Myself* (New York: Harper & Brothers, 1959), p. 227.
70. *Christian Leader*, December 1, 1934, pp. 1510-1512; December 8, 1934, pp. 1546-1548; Gaines, pp. 55, 111-112, 117-118 (based in part on John Murray Atwood, *Christian Leader*, October 1949, p. 352); A. Seaburg, op. cit.; Miller, op. cit., p. 500.
71. Skinner, *Liberalism Faces the Future* (New York: Macmillan, 1937), pp. 6-7.
72. Skinner, *Human Nature and the Nature of Evil* (Boston: Universalist Publishing House, 1939), pp. 59, 90, 148, 161.
73. James D. Hunt, unpublished analysis.
74. Skinner and Alfred S. Cole, *Hell's Ramparts Fell* (Boston: Universalist Publishing House, 1941); Gaines, p. 105.
75. Gaines, p. 115 (based on *Tufts College Catalogue*, 1938-39); Howe, interview with McKeeman.

76. Gaines, pp. 115-116 (based on interview with C. A. S.).
77. Gaines, pp. 68-69 (based in part on letter, Eugene Adams to Gaines, July 19, 1960).
78. Gaines, p. 129 (based on interview with Alfred S. Cole); Miller, op. cit., p. 500.
79. Skinner, *A Religion for Greatness* (Boston: Universalist Publishing House, 1945, reprinted 1958); Gaines, p. 23 (based on Pink *et al.*, op. cit., pp. 233-234), pp. 103-107.
80. Skinner, *A Religion for Greatness*, pp. 11, 12, 13.
81. Ibid., pp. 52-53 (cited in Gaines, pp. 105-106).
82. Ibid., p. 121.
83. See James D. Hunt, "The Liberal Theology of Clarence R. Skinner," *Journal of the Universalist Historical Society*, Vol. VII, 1967-68, pp. 102-120 (reprinted in this book) for a critical analysis of Skinner's thought.
84. Charles A. Howe, "Clinton Lee Scott, Revitalizer of Universalism," *Proceedings of the Unitarian Universalist Historical Society*, Vol. XXI, Part II, 1989, pp. 9-10.
85. Skinner, *Worship and a Well Ordered Life* (Boston: Universalist Historical Society and Meeting House Press, 1955); Gaines, pp. 129-131 (based on interview with C. A. S.).
86. Gaines, pp. 131-132 (based on interview with C. A. S.); Miller, op. cit., p. 500.
87. Gaines, p. 133 (based on interview with C. A. S.).
88. Gaines, pp. 133-134 (based on interview with C. A. S.; and letter, Alfred S. Cole to Alan Seaburg, February 20, 1956, Universalist Historical Society files); Miller, op. cit., p. 500; A. Seaburg, op. cit., p. 77.
89. See particularly Volume V (1964-65) and Volume VII (1967-68).
90. "Resolution on the Death of Clarence Russell Skinner," Universalist Historical Society files (cited in Gaines, pp. 134-135).

The Liberal Theology of
Clarence R. Skinner

James D. Hunt

Clarence R. Skinner has been celebrated as a man, as a teacher, and as a leader of Universalist social consciousness. Little study has been made of his theology, although his five books and many articles represent the most comprehensive and sustained defense of liberalism by any Universalist in the first half of the twentieth century.

Skinner was a man of vision, and his vision was of the unity of the human race. He had a conception of universalism that had far-reaching theological and social implications, a conception that plays a major role in Unitarian Universalist theology today. This study will present the main outlines of his view of liberalism, of religion, of the relation of Christianity to universalism, and of the church.

First, a brief review of his career. He was born in 1881 in Brooklyn, where his father was an editor of the *Brooklyn Eagle*. The Skinner family had long been active in Universalist religious and educational affairs. He graduated from St. Lawrence University as a Phi Beta Kappa in 1904. After pastorates in New York City, Mt. Vernon, New York, and Lowell, Massachusetts, he was appointed Assistant Professor of Applied Christianity at Crane Theological School in 1914, becoming Dean in 1933 and retiring in 1945. He died in 1949.

As a young minister he was active in the social gospel movement and became secretary of the Universalist Social

Service Commission. He wrote a small book, *The Social Impli-cations of Universalism*, in 1915, and was the chief author of the "Declaration of Social Principles" adopted by the Univer-salists in 1917. He was a pacifist and was much disheartened by the war, and after it established the Community Church of Boston, of which he was the "leader"—not the minister—until 1936.[1] He was close intellectually and professionally to John Haynes Holmes. The Community Church of Boston was modeled on the New York venture, and both Holmes and his colleague, John Herman Randall, Jr., journeyed fre-quently to Boston to speak. His major books were written in the 1930s and 40s. There was a volume of sermons from the pulpit of the Community Church, entitled *A Free Pulpit in Action* (1931). In the late thirties appeared two defenses of religious liberalism, *Liberalism Faces the Future* (1937) and *Human Nature and the Nature of Evil* (1939). At the close of the war, *A Religion for Greatness* appeared (1945), and the Universalist Historical Society issued a posthumous collec-tion of three manuscripts under the title *Worship and a Well Ordered Life* (1955).

Liberalism

In his major statement on liberalism, *Liberalism Faces the Future*, issued in 1937 at a time when liberalism was under attack from many quarters, he saw liberalism as a certain type of relationship to authority. The book was originally a lecture series given at Star Island [Conference Center near Ports-mouth, New Hampshire], entitled "The Function of Liberal-ism in a World of Rising Authorities," and when he seeks to define liberalism it is by contrast to "illiberalism," which is "submission to authority because it is authority." Liberalism, he says, "recognizes the place of authority but . . . challenges it." The liberal is one with the innovators, the explorers, the inventors. "Liberalism means the emancipated mind, the hun-ger for new experiences."[2]

Skinner uses a significant metaphor when he speaks of the genesis of the liberal attitude: "Liberalism began as soon as man dared to trust his own faculties and to insist upon his right to think out the problems of life for himself." Liberalism is thus an element in maturation, in man's coming of age. Where have we heard this language before? It is the voice of Enlightenment. Immanuel Kant, in his essay of 1795, "What Is Enlightenment?" used nearly identical words: "Enlightenment is escape from self-inflicted immaturity." It represented the overcoming of tradition by the inner authority of reason. We have also heard this language more recently. The image of man daring to use his own faculties is exploited by Harvey Cox in the opening sentence of *The Secular City*: "We have defined secularization as the liberation of man from religious and metaphysical tutelage, the turning of his attention away from other worlds and toward this one." What Skinner calls liberalism, Kant called Enlightenment, and Cox calls secularization. In each instance there is an image of maturity, of man taking charge of his own affairs, and of arbitrary authority standing between man and the full development of his being. Like John Dewey and others of his time, Skinner makes use of the images of the scientist and the pioneer to symbolize the liberal. Like the pioneer the liberal pushes out into the unknown. Like the scientist the liberal refuses to rely on tradition but makes a fresh examination of data, and contributes to the cumulative development of truth. One of Skinner's favorite contrasts is drawn between "a thoroughgoing traditionalist, bound by precedent," and "a free spirit, delving into research. . . ."[3] The researcher is the representative of liberalism in action.

In his liberalism, Skinner makes no clear distinction between religion and politics. When he speaks of religious liberalism, he passes easily from the inner life of the individual to social planning. Political liberalism, or the social gospel, is of a piece with religious liberalism for him. The liberalism that faces the future is both political and religious; and life must be unified. The trouble with many liberals, he asserts, is that they do not go all the way with their liberalism. This is the message contained in the title of his first book, *The Social Implications of Universalism*: universalism is an idea which has both religious implications and social implications. The elements of the liberal philosophy were clearly stated by Skinner himself in these words:

> A starting point in the liberal philosophy is belief in man. Implied in every Emancipation and reform is the truth that man is working for and that at the core of human nature is a something sound and good.[4]
>
> Those who have this confidence in man—in his intelligence, his moral capacity, and his power to solve problems—will not appeal to an outward and artificial authority. Rather they will believe that inherent in men there lies the truth; involved in human nature are powers and capacities adequate to the situation. The authority which a liberal seeks is *within*.[5]

Religion

There was a powerful streak of mysticism in Skinner which influenced both his theology and his sociology. It was a deep consciousness of the oneness of things. His favorite summation of the nature of religion was that "it provides insight into the unities and universals," and we shall examine the terms of this definition.

First, insight. A religious philosophy based on insight or intuition should be familiar to the heirs of the transcendentalists. Skinner uses the terms "insight," "intuition," and "mysticism" interchangeably. The term "insight" or "intuition," meaning a direct perception of the inner nature of a thing, suggests that religion is an experience which implies an external reality whose nature is being apprehended, and there is a quality of value seen in that reality. "Religion," he wrote, "means to me the reverent attitude to whatever seems to the worshipper the greatest and the best."[6]

Such an intuitive philosophy of religion, with strong value-tones, is based on man's sensitivity and capacity for religious knowledge and implies a validation of religious sensitivity by moral earnestness. It provided an effective base for moral action, and in the form of the social gospel it gave a transcendent dimension to reform.

Skinner stresses the importance of remaining open to insight. Worship is for him the process of attaining insight, and becomes religiously significant by its fulfillment of this function. Worship he regarded as that "natural form of behavior" which man exhibits in the presence of an object of value which he seeks to attain:

> Worship exists wherever there is tension between the individual and an object which he reverently holds to be of highest significance and value. It is the outreach of man to attain union with this object—to know it, to feel it, to experience it.[7]

Worship precedes religion. Worship is the experience, religion the crystallized deposit of experience. Here Skinner makes use of the familiar contrast between original experience and habit which may be seen, for example, in Emerson. The original experience is reality, while habit is the empty shell. Life is seen as a process of experience leading to habit formation, with fresh experience being the creative and energizing possibility in every situation. For Skinner, worship was such an occasion of fresh possibility, it was "the craving for a reality which transcends our daily experience."[8] This "reality" of which Skinner spoke gives evidence that here is no mere subjectivity in religion; there is an external as well as an internal reality which must be taken into account. "Religious experience is real," he insists, and goes on to assert, "the experience of worship implies an object in the environment."[9] Here Skinner definitely moves beyond subjectivism and positivistic humanism. Drawing a contrast between "radical religion," which goes to the root of the matter, and superficial religion, which does not, he sees radical religion entailing some sort of metaphysical realism. It gets down to fundamentals, and the fundamentals are real. Skinner, without hesitation, would use the word "God" to denote the final reality of being and value. God is "the symbol of all man's highest ideals," "the summation of all values."[10] But lest it be thought that God is merely human value, Skinner is explicit in his metaphysical reference: "I profoundly believe, with my whole heart and mind, that there is a creative power at the center of the whole universe evolving law and order on a majestic scale."[11] His God does not seem to have personal qualities, but it is more than value; it has ontological status.

Yet value is a central element in Skinner's apprehension of the nature of religion. Religion is an active spiritual relation, an aspiration, a movement toward value, and for this reason it issues in moral insight and commitment. The social implications of religion are not tacked on later; they are in the original religious experience itself, and their dimensions are seen in the often repeated phrase, "the unities and the universals." A focus on the unities and universals might seem to be merely a clever phrase for use by Unitarians and Universalists, but for Skinner it had definite mystical and ethical significance, and was rightly employed as the summation of his religious philosophy.

By "unity" Skinner means "the coherence of what may seem to be separate, into a oneness, an operative harmony, a functional relationship which belongs to all the parts of a whole."[12] Notice that it suggests an imaginative perception of an inner identity which may not appear at first sight; once more we are talking about insight and intuition. Here the intuition is of the unified or organic or functionally interdependent character of reality. A curious feature of Skinner's language at this point is that although he defines "unity," he usually speaks of "the unities" in the plural. I think this is because he is recurrently at the point of asserting certain relationships which are apparent to him but not so readily apparent to his audience: especially the unity between faith and social reform, and the functional interdependence of the human community. He finds himself asserting repeatedly that such a unity exists, that Universalism has social implications, and that the Universalist cannot be unified unless he attains insight into this relationship.

With the unities are paired the universals. "Universal" is a term which for Skinner means the absence of limits; it is a negative term in that it means limitlessness, or, as he says, "the antithesis of the limited, . . . the opposite of the partial. . . . When we speak of universalism we shall mean a philosophy of life or system of values which stresses the largest possible Weltanschauung, or world outlook, in contrast to the narrow view which is herein denominated partialism."[13] The unities and the universals thus are a set of functionally cooperative terms: unity is a positive attribute of things, while universalism is a removal of all limits to unity. The unities refer to things as they truly are; the universals refer to things as they ought to be.

In Skinner's hands, the conception of religion as insight into the unities and universals provides a flexible and subtle tool for theology and ethics. He draws upon it to redefine the Christian faith in terms of moral idealism with an inclusiveness of scope which is worldwide and even cosmic in proportions. Let us illustrate this with a fairly representative passage, this one from Skinner's essay on "What Religion Means to Me," published in the *Tufts Papers on Religion* in 1939:

> . . . the soul is restless until it has moved out to the uttermost boundaries of the universe. It will be satisfied with nothing less than the whole of reality. It feels kinship with atoms, persons, social movements, and galaxies of stars wheeling in silent majesty across infinitudes of space. This is the highest reach of the human intellect, this is the profoundest reality of the

human soul, this is the greatest and best man can know. It is symbolized by the great word "God," but the word is not the reality. It is the experience that counts. Man is caught up into a sublimity that lifts him, liberates his deepest self, stretches his imagination till it touches east and west, includes high and low, inspires and enriches him. This is the ultimate religion. In the great words of the poet Coleridge:

"'Tis the sublime of man, his noon-tide majesty,

To know himself parts and proportions of one wondrous whole."

To me the highest type of religious experience is that which gives man a sense of unity and universality. Most of our life is spent in narrow segments. Our horizon is hemmed about by kitchen walls, office desks, narrow prejudices of race, class or creed. In religion, these partialisms, broken fragments of life, are lifted into a vast and profound oneness. Our littleness becomes stretched to cosmic greatness.[14]

His vivid homiletic style is apparent in this passage, as is his identification of personal unification with the conceptual unification of science and religion. The quotation from Coleridge is also characteristic; the romantic poets dot his pages.

We have been speaking of the unities and universals as if religion were for Skinner chiefly a conceptual enterprise; but the passage just quoted reminds us that "it is the experience that counts," and Skinner in fact gives much attention to the phenomenon of faith.

Faith, he used to say, is "belief plus,"[15] and the plus was power, "that force which carries belief into action."[16] Over and over again faith is spoken of as a form of energy: it is "the greatest creative force in the history of man," it "turns potentialities into actualities." "Whenever man has triumphed over apparently insuperable obstacles, wherever he has wrung secrets from the unknown, wherever he has achieved the ideal,—there and then he has employed faith."[17] In this sense faith provides the dynamic by which religious insight may achieve moral articulation, but there is a second sense of the word in Skinner's usage, and in this sense faith is a name for the insight itself. In this second use of the word, the plus in "belief plus" is not power as the power to act, but power as the power to see: it is the attainment of insight. "By faith we send our vision beyond the actual and the seen into the realm of what may be the profoundly real."[18] Here Skinner sees a vital connection between the attainment of vision and the attainment of power. The power of faith derives from the power of its conception of reality.

If faith is a power, however, it can be badly used, misused, and misdirected, like any other power, and Skinner warns repeatedly against uncritical reliance upon belief. Superstition is one form of uncritical belief, a form which derives particularly from not keeping up to date. Myth, which today is an honorable word in the theological vocabulary, represented for Skinner merely a prescientific primitivism, the acceptance of belief without empirical verification. Likewise the power of faith could be dangerous: "Religious emotions and enthusiasms may be made to serve either intolerant fear or the lovely life of peace and healing good will."[19]

What brings faith under control? Reason does; it provides the definition of the ends which religious emotions must serve, just as myth must be brought under the discipline of advancing science. "The glory of religion is that it seeks the unseen and the unknown, but what is virtue under certain conditions of restraint and understanding may easily become vice under conditions of unrestraint and unguided emotionalism."[20] Reason provides the guidance, and it operates by "integrating religion into the rest of life" by means of inculcating "a universal point of view."[21] Here the unities and universals return, this time as the content of a rational view of life that provides guidance for the power of faith. Faith when it is linked with reason, an insight into the unities and universals which has a power of commitment behind it, is for Skinner the element which has the right and the capacity to transform the world, and it is this capacity which Universalism especially ought to generate.

A unique concept underlying Skinner's theology is "social mysticism," a term which provides a critical key to understanding the junction between religion and ethics. He expressed it this way:

> If there is anything which ought to be distinctive of religion, it is a feeling of active relationship between the self and a mystic, other, better world. There is no reason why this sense of relationship should be confined to a hazy realm which the soul visits after death. Can there not be a social and political mysticism which calls forth an eager faith? Can we not visualize another better world which is not yet real, but is capable of becoming a reality? The old mysticism was individualistic. But this other mysticism would contain a *diviner urge* and *lay upon man a sense of something great to be done.* Not to die for our faith as the saint of old, not to kill for it, as does the soldier, but [something] *to live for*—to live splendidly, with utter devotion. Under its impulse man would live generously, bravely, with the sense of youth eager for strange quests and delighting in divine surprise.[22]

There are several images fused here: the mystic in love with God, the revolutionist in love with destiny, the savior in love with man. Social mysticism was the Kingdom of God, the revolution, the brotherhood of man, all in one. It was a joining of the universal spiritual vision with the universally inclusive ethical imperative. It was "the social implication of universalism," and it was the final meaning of religion as "insight into the unities and universals."

Christianity

Skinner in his writings seems always to have identified himself as a Christian. To him there seems to have been no great difference between Christianity and Universalism as he understood them. In his last published article he wrote:

> What shall we say of Christianity? We are so completely in it and of it that it is hard, if not impossible, to gain historical perspective. . . . What we think and say about Christianity is conditioned by habit and the will to believe. . . . We honor it by word reaction, but do we honestly have so profound a faith in it that we dare to live it in our personal lives, or do we actually want to see it practiced in the world at large?[23]

While he implied criticism here, it is a criticism of Christianity as lived, rather than Christianity as a faith.

Yet in two of his major books he hardly ever mentioned Christianity except to draw a few historical illustrations from it. In 1937 "liberalism" was the object of his concern, and in 1945 it was "a religion for greatness," or Universalism. While he could rank himself with Christianity without difficulty in his own mind, he did not see Christianity in terms of a distinctive or unique revelation of religious truth. No, Christianity was a form of religion, and Skinner was especially conscious that it was an *old* form of religion.

More fundamental than Christianity was religion. Religion was man's consciousness of his relatedness to being, his dependence upon the cosmos and his unity with his fellow man. Religion was the religious experience, and Christianity, whatever its value in the past, was now significant to the extent that it could serve as a means for generating the religious experience, the sense of oneness, in men.

"Shall we free Christianity from the encumbrances which crush its spirit?" he asked. It was bound and hampered by its view of a closed universe, which implied a closed revelation and a static view of truth. Its great need was to be "brought up to date so that it squares with our concept of reality," he demanded, setting forth a program for the revitalization of theology:

> Today we must accept the dynamic concept of life. To us moderns there are no closed systems in the heavens or on the earth. All is in flux and we must apply the law of evolution to all religious tenets. God, revelation, saviour and salvation must be interpreted as changing with a developing universe. Nothing is finished, not even God. The Bible is a continuing library. Christ is one of a long line of redeemers. Christian theology is not final or absolute, but is to be added to, subtracted from, and developed in the light of what we shall learn in the future.[24]

Concerning the figure of Jesus he observed, and this in 1914, "The modern interest in Christ is pragmatic rather than dogmatic." He saw Jesus as a moral teacher, a visionary, an emancipator whose message was the Fatherhood of God and the Brotherhood of Man, and whose vision was the Kingdom of God. It was his universal vision, recovered for our time as the social gospel, which should be the center of Christianity. But Christianity had separated Christ from his principles. For centuries the theologians wrangled over the person of Christ and almost completely forgot his program. "Christ the person became exalted above and away from Christianity, the program, and the world thus lost the power which, if generally accepted, might have saved it from the long list of miseries and woes which have cursed it."[25]

It is the message of Christ which for Skinner is more fundamental than his person, and it is the message of Christianity which is more fundamental than its form. The message is "the fatherhood of God and the brotherhood of man," as he would say in 1914, or it is "the religion for greatness," as he would say in 1945. In either event, it was a thrust toward a universal consciousness with social implications, a social gospel, an inclusive religion of universalism. The universal, the inclusive, the unifying—this is the real meaning of Christianity for Skinner, and it is a religion that must abjure all that separates and divides.

Universalism, then, is his theme, and Universalism is the criterion and norm for Christianity. Insofar as Christianity affirms the inclusive and the universal, insofar as it leads to a wider unity, it is the hope of man, but insofar as Christianity or any other faith divides men into sectarian communities and fosters narrowness and hostility, it is to be overcome.

Thus Skinner's universalism, even at the turn of the century, placed Christianity on a par with all the other religions—what was good in Christianity was also what was of value in the other religions, and the sins of Christian exclusiveness were the sins of other great religions also. The element of greatest value in a religion was, for Skinner, not the particular, the unique, as a generation of [Karl] Barth-inspired theologians have taught us, but the universal. The traditions divide, but religion is one, he would insist. Religion is man's consciousness of the unities and the universals. In the great liberal tradition of [Friedrich] Schleiermacher, [Samuel Taylor] Coleridge, and [Ralph Waldo] Emerson, the great human fact and the ground of human hope is the capacity of man to sense his relatedness to all that exists. It is a theology unabashedly constructed on man's religiousness, which he calls Faith.

Unlike Emerson, whose "Divinity School Address" called for a religion of intuition but ended by commending traditional forms in worship, Skinner took seriously the Concord seer's word that "faith makes its own forms." Emerson had written, "Rather let the breath of new life be breathed by you through the forms already existing," but Skinner in his philosophy of worship called for a "wise, mature revolt" against old forms. In his manuscript on "Worship" (published posthumously by this [Historical] Society and the Meeting House Press), Skinner set forth a philosophy of the relation of form to meaning in worship which relied upon the Emersonian distinction between imitation and originality. He saw three possibilities: the classicists, who retain old meanings in old forms, the compromising modernists, who put new meaning in old forms, and the radicals, who seek new forms to express new meanings. The radicals, like the classicists, are thoroughgoing in their desire for a unity of form and meaning; Skinner calls them "conscientious objectors" to compromise. "These radicals . . . simply cannot accept the orthodox retreat into the past or the modernist's compromise with consistency. Their minds do not work in the devious ways of symbolism, and they demand a clear-cut, definitive statement of what, to them, is true." Furthermore, they see new spiritual values arising in the present, and would have their worship grasp these new realities. "The creative religionist," he writes, "insists that the materials for a real experience of worship abound in our present culture. . . . The old forms symbolizing an ancient impulse cannot give adequate expression to this pulsating, passionate life of ours."[26]

Whereas Skinner called for a religion which makes use of the materials of contemporary culture, similar words and concepts were employed by Kenneth Patton in an effort to establish a worship which draws not only from contemporary culture, but from the art and traditions of all the great religions of mankind as well. Kenneth Patton cooperated with the Historical Society in publishing Skinner's manuscript on worship, and printed parts of it in his own short-lived "journal for developing liberal religious thought," *The Edge*. Mr. Patton's Berry Street Lecture for 1965, proposing "plenitude of being" as a focal concept for liberal religion, showed a theology resonating closely with Skinner's at many points. The fundamental conception has cosmic, personal, and social dimensions, Patton said, and "the key principle underlying the social plenitude of being is universality, the principle of all-inclusiveness." He asks, "Can a person extend his understanding and sympathies to all peoples . . . ?" and answers, "It can be done. The question is only whether we have the intelligence, the compassion, the motivation to achieve the concept of humanity within us. . . . This ideal . . . does not depart from the universal salvation of Universalism but only translates it from the realms of immortality and theology into the lives we live in this world. . . . This ideal is in the tradition of our twin themes of unity and universality."[27]

Patton here sounds strikingly like Skinner, and there is much in common between Patton's naturalistic mysticism and Skinner's social mysticism. Patton's thrust toward an exclusive religious expression, while more appreciative of tradition and of the aesthetic dimension in worship than was Skinner, nevertheless exhibits the essential character of universalism as Skinner envisioned it. For both men, the great spiritual fact which our times have laid bare is the unity of the human race, and religion which fails to come to grips with this fact is simply inadequate and furthermore is dangerous. "Man must enlarge the borders of his consciousness to include the human race"[28]; these words of Skinner's could well be the creed of [Boston's] Charles Street Meeting House.

The Church

Skinner's view of the church was set forth in a series of lectures given at the occasion of the founding of the Community Church in Boston in 1920. After his death, these were published as "The Church as a Universal Community," the first of the three selections in the book, *Worship and a Well Ordered Life*. The title, "The Church as a Universal Community," aptly suggests Skinner's conception in its major dimensions.

1. *Church*. The most needed institution of all was a church, if only because of the power of science and technology which needed to be harnessed to the service of the community. "It is apparent that there must be an integration of science with

life," he wrote. "It must soon become dominated by an authoritative and commanding passion to contribute to the common good, or it will utterly destroy civilization." Immense social forces also cried for integration. "Therefore the dominant need of the age is the creation of spiritual power great enough to moralize our mechanisms, to integrate them into a new world scheme which shall secure the solidarity of all men."[29] With some trepidation, because of the fossilized character of institutionalized religion, but also with some hope because of the creative and aspiring nature of man, Skinner looked to religion to provide the new integrating vision.

Especially it was to be a church because Skinner held that a chief defect of liberal Christianity and of Christianity generally was its excessive individualism; he called for the replacement of the old individualistic mysticism with a new social mysticism promising not the salvation of the individual after death, but the creation of a better world. A social mysticism implied a social institution; a church as the vehicle for the religious vision.

2. *Universal.* The church was to be universal in its vision and inclusive in its membership. Skinner suggested that the unity and diversity which characterized a college might serve as a model for the church. In a college a variety of purposes, methods, and philosophies are not only present but encouraged. The church, he felt, should exhibit this same inclusiveness. Its ministry, he felt, should be diverse, with "a faculty of leaders"[30] and a variety of forms of meeting for worship, study, and action. He was keenly aware of the many groups who had ceased to have interest in the church, among them labor, the intelligentsia, those interested in psychotherapy and "new thought," the youth, and he also saw the declining proportion of men and the lack of contact between Protestantism and the foreigner. Each of these groups had its own contribution, which by its departure was lost to the church: Skinner was aware here of the diversity of human groups, and of the relation between social groups and values. These particular

groups which had been lost to the church seem to be exactly the groups which were most needed, because of what they had contributed. The revitalization of the church, he said "must come from the classes and groups which are forming the spiritual values of the future,"[31] and one could interpret the design of the Community Church as an effort to identify and form a working fellowship of just those value-creating classes.

3. *Community.* Josiah Royce had written, "The future task of religion is the task of inventing and applying arts which shall win men over to unity. . . . Judge every social device, every proposed reform, every national and every local enterprise, by the one test: does this help towards the coming of the universal community?"[32] Skinner cited this passage in illustration of the centrality of the idea of community for his vision of the church. Community was the goal, and community was the unifying idea of his church. "The function of the community church," he wrote, "is to provide a new basis for the unity of religious life in substituting the community idea for the theological idea as its chief rallying point."[33] The community idea served him still further by suggesting a second model for his church, namely, the community center. Like a community center, the church should express the common idealism and diversity of interests of a whole neighborhood of people. Like a community center, a church should derive its program not from tradition but from the interests and the needs of the present. Like a community center, a church should offer help to its people in raising their sights and developing their capacities to relate to society on a higher level.

These were his models. In his words, "Is it unreasonable to hope that in time the church might be organized as effectively as the college, and that religion might attain as creative and spontaneous an expression in the neighborhood, as life is expressed in the Community Center?"[34] In his lectures for 1920 he set forth a detailed conception of the religious community center at work, and in the preface to his volume of sermons from the Community Church published in 1931, he gave a description of the preaching, the worship, and the activities of that church in its first decade.

These are the major directions of Skinner's theology: Liberalism as man thinking for himself; Religion as insight into the unities and universals; Christianity as a form of the emerging universal religion; and the Church as a universal community.

Criticisms

Before leaving Skinner, a few things must be said in criticism of the man and his work. If we are to see him in perspective and if we are to learn from him anything about ourselves, we must focus on his limitations and failures as well as upon his achievements.

Certain aspects of Skinner's style are immediately disappointing to the critical reader. His is essentially a hortatory or homiletical style, full of aphorisms but short on sustained analysis and surprisingly weak when analysis is attempted. His sentences ring with earnestness and the power of his personality, and his intense idealism vibrates through them, but at the points where one most wishes Skinner to provide concrete guidance, it often seems that he has not done his homework. The many chapters of *A Religion for Greatness* which apply the central insights of a universalistic outlook to social issues are disappointing from a man noted as a professor of sociology and social ethics. The chapters on "Economic Universalism," "Racial Universalism," "Political Universalism," "Social Universalism," and "Scientific Universalism" are all full of unfounded assertions, unsupported generalizations, and turn out to be very vague programmatically. One striking example from *A Religion for Greatness* is, "Poverty must be abolished. . . . If we don't do it one way, we shall do it another."[35] It would be very difficult to build a poverty program on such advice. This is not to ridicule Skinner, by any means. His attention to issues and to gathering the facts on specific cases was serious. His early reports on the Sacco-

Vanzetti case, for instance, were cited in a recent scholarly study as "the soundest discussion of the case in this first crucial year."[36] But when it came to developing a theoretical picture of what must be done and how ethical imperatives relate to concrete proposals, he failed to give much guidance in his books.

One may justly criticize Skinner's scholarship in other respects, too. His use of history was notoriously weak, and full of errors, some of which were due to carelessness and others due to ignorance. His grasp of sociological and psychological theory was rudimentary and his knowledge of theology and philosophy was thin. Yet this was the dean of one of our theological schools, and one of the few Universalists to attempt to make a comprehensive statement of the Universalist position and a defense of liberalism in an age when liberalism was on the run. No wonder Universalism failed to gain the respect of men of intelligence and education! If this was the level of its scholarship, there was little promise here of serious encounter with thought.

What Skinner did have was a vision and a set of ideals which were in a great tradition and represented an important new interpretation of that tradition. We have suggested some of the outlines of that vision, and shall, in conclusion, say some things concerning its significance. But before passing too far from this critical stance toward Skinner, we must examine some serious deficiencies of his vision and some extremely questionable teachings which were not merely peripheral to his vision but which were integral to it.

The first of these questionable teachings of Skinner's was his reliance, from beginning to end, upon a conception of cultural and religious evolution. The serious criticism of the doctrine of progress which occupied the attention of so many men during his lifetime never really touched him. In his final writings he was almost as optimistic in his expressions and every bit as optimistic in his basic theory as he was in the beginning. He believed that history exhibited a steady growth from partialism toward universalism. History was his ground of hope. This evolutionary optimism meant that for him the criterion for authenticity in theology turned out to be modernity. That which was up-to-date was more authentic than anything which was old. When he came to analyze forms of worship, for example, he saw three approaches to the problem of worship: old meanings in old forms, new meanings in old forms, and new meanings in new forms, and it was the last which was the best. That the values of the present are by nature better than the values of the past is a dubious assumption at best, and in some instances a dangerous one. Skinner, like many of his age, was preoccupied with the problem of overcoming the dead hand of tradition, and he saw rebellion as anti-traditionalism. Consequently, in one of his last writings he could make what seems today a very curious statement indeed: "The uncompromising rebel says that modern man must adjust his entire self to the new meanings and values which characterize our age."[37] Adjusting the entire self to the values of the age sounds more like a recipe for conformity than rebelliousness, of which I shall say more in a moment.

A second questionable teaching which is to be found especially in Skinner's writings on worship and individual psychology is what is best known as "positive thinking," or "Pealeism" [the philosophy of Norman Vincent Peale, a popular preacher and writer in the 1940s and 1950s]. Skinner the social prophet had a very dubious psychology, stressing the value of belief *per se* and asserting that the act of belief is part of good mental health. "Faith in God," he asserts, ". . . makes for a life of calm composure. It is hygienic for body and soul. It prevents breakdowns which come upon those who lose all confidence in the universe, and those lives are set adrift."[38] Earlier in this same essay ("A Well Ordered Life") he gives three recommendations for finding inner resources. They are (1) "the constant assertion to oneself that we are capable of more strength and power than we have ever developed," (2) meditation on the realities of inner power, so that "their meaning will sink into your subconsciousness and eventually will become a part of the conscious resources of your daily existence," and (3) "Finally, action. Do something to prove your strength," and develop habits of self-mastery by beginning with small tasks and working up.[39] Now, this is really a very ordinary kind of self-persuasion and mind-cure technique, and it is disappointing to find Skinner descending to the level of Peale's positive thinking. Unfortunately, one fails to find evidence that his psychology ever rose much above this level. He asserted from the beginning that the person could be healed by thinking right thoughts, and what those right thoughts were could be determined from a third quality of his system.

The third dubious doctrine is Skinner's totalistic conception of universalism. Consider such statements as these from *A Religion for Greatness*: "We are so made that we function most efficiently when we are coordinated with others of our kind"; "The more complete the integration, the more the psychic and social well-being."[40] Skinner lays great stress on the integration of the individual with the whole, the coordination of elements of society, the unifying vision. "There must be a new passion entering the lives of mankind," he wrote, "fusing them into a coordinated whole."[41] Here is the social program of his social mysticism; it is a totalistic vision, in which the unity of the whole provides moral direction for the parts, and inclusiveness is the prime value. "Is not maturity," he asks, "largely a matter of discovering the nexus which binds together all forms of reality in the entire universe?"[42] In reading these passages, one gets the impression that Skinner would be hard put to understand Thoreau. Skinner's model for selfhood is the self given over to a social passion for the sake of augmenting the growing unity of the human race. Universalism as he presents it is an overcoming of partialism, and one may well fear that it may be an overcoming of particularity and uniqueness, an overcoming of privacy and inwardness as well. Nor is one reassured in this fear by Skinner's own statements concerning individuals and their value, for he also says, in *A*

Religion for Greatness, "Man's existence and destiny as an individual (that is as a separate unit) are a form of restriction and limitation. Separateness is an imprisonment. We find the meaning of human personality and the meaning of the whole universe in the unity of the parts with the whole."[43]

It is hardly necessary to point out the inadequacy of such a doctrine. However meaningful Skinner's unifying vision, we must see that something is severely wrong in a theological position that defines the distinctiveness and uniqueness of the individual in primarily negative terms, and identifies particularity with partialism and calls it sin. He was, however inconsistently, insistent on the protection of minority views, and loved to quote Charles Fleischer's definition of democracy as "the organization of society with respect to the individual." Respect to the individual he intended, and fought for, but if we look to him also for theology, we find that unfortunately he has a theology which only with difficulty gives respect to the individual.

These weaknesses of Skinner's work, his evolutionism, his Pealeism, and his societism, are serious weaknesses, and they are exactly the weaknesses in liberal evolutionary idealism that existentialist theology seeks to overcome. When reading Skinner at these points, we are reading a voice out of the past, a voice from an age when the major theological problem was the conflict between static tradition and evolutionary emergence, when the incorporation of the scientific mode of thinking was the bright new frontier of theology. In many ways we have not met these requirements yet, but theology has long since turned to new issues: the problems of mass movements and culture religions, the problems of power and the loss of identity, the problems of a nightmare future rather than the problems of an emerging new age of hope being realized.

Conclusions

We can hardly condemn Skinner for confronting the issues of his time instead of the issues of our time. If he was unprepared to confront certain questions, we must acknowledge that, and be aware also that to the extent our theology follows his, we too may be unprepared to deal with some of these same issues.

At other and more pertinent points, Skinner's theology offers some commanding directions which we can ignore only at our peril and which indicate the real strength and depth of the man.

First, Skinner never ceased to insist that the power of religion was located in its universal vision. The theological inclusiveness which took a faith in man as its starting point recognized the validity of the religions of man, and offered its own rational criterion for the validity of religion: inclusiveness, or universalism.

Second, Skinner never ceased to insist that universalism had social implications. Inclusiveness was his ethical keynote, and he often observed that secular movements and institutions were far more ethical in this respect than was religion. In his social ethics Skinner saw the secular offering to religion a health-giving call to inclusiveness and to the reality of dealing with living concerns.

Third, Skinner saw the religious meaning of the here-and-now. In his constant critique of tradition, he affirmed the creative uses of the contemporary and called for the restructuring of thought, of worship, and of the church in terms of present needs and opportunities. He identified the present moment and its thrust toward the future as the meaningful occasion of work.

Let Clarence Skinner have the last word:

There are two alternatives, and only two, before us. First, which is unlikely, is that we unscramble our modern interdependent culture, returning to separate and isolationist lives. If we went back to the village stage of existence, then we might be partialists to our hearts' content. Such a world would not *demand* greatness.

The other alternative is so to expand our spiritual powers that we vastly increase the range of our understanding and sympathy. There is no middle way. It is greatness—universalism—or perish.[44]

Notes

1. See Charles A. Gaines, "Clarence Skinner: Image of a Movement," BD Thesis, Crane Theological School, 1961; and "Clarence R. Skinner: The Dark Years," *Journal of the Universalist Historical Society*, III (1962), 1-13.
2. *Liberalism Faces the Future* (New York: Macmillan, 1937), p. 5.
3. Ibid., p. 6.
4. Ibid., p. 57.
5. Ibid., p. 64.
6. "What Religion Means to Me," *Tufts Papers on Religion* (Boston: Universalist Publishing House, 1939), p. 9.
7. *Worship and a Well Ordered Life* (Boston: Universalist Historical Society and Meeting House Press, 1955), p. 66.
8. Ibid., p. 70.
9. Ibid., p. 78.
10. Ibid., pp. 70 ff.
11. Ibid., p. 173.
12. *A Religion for Greatness* (Boston: Universalist Publishing House, 1945), p. 16.
13. Ibid.
14. "What Religion Means to Me," pp. 13 ff.
15. *Liberalism Faces the Future*, p. 158.
16. "Superstition, Reason, and Faith," pamphlet edition (reprinted from the *Christian Leader*, Nov. 16 and Dec. 2, 1946), p. 11.
17. Ibid., p. 15.
18. Ibid., p. 13. In a climactic passage in *A Religion for Greatness*, the two uses of the word are laid down side by side: "Faith is a kind of courage which makes it possible to put our belief into action.

It is an act of creative imagination which gives us an insight into the nature of the unseen." p. 114.

19. "What Religion Means to Me," p. 14.
20. "Superstition, Reason, and Faith," p. 7.
21. "What Religion Means to Me," pp. 14 ff.
22. *Worship and a Well Ordered Life*, p. 14, reconstructed with the help of the editor, Alfred S. Cole. Charles A. Gaines argues in his thesis ("Clarence Skinner: Image of a Movement," pp. 106-108) that Skinner eventually gave up the social gospel for mysticism, but this seems doubtful since Skinner's final articles were concerned with social issues, and the concept of "social mysticism" may be found in some form throughout his work from beginning to end.
23. "The World of Tomorrow," *Christian Leader*, June 19, 1948.
24. "Superstition, Reason, and Faith," p. 8.
25. *The Social Implications of Universalism*, as reprinted in the *Annual Journal of the Universalist Historical Society*, V (1964-65), pp. 109-110.
26. *Worship and a Well Ordered Life*, pp. 126, 134-135.
27. Kenneth L. Patton, "Plenitude of Being," *Journal of the Liberal Ministry*, V, 3 (Fall 1965), pp. 141-144.
28. *A Religion for Greatness*, p. 70.
29. *Worship and a Well Ordered Life*, pp. 1, 3.
30. Ibid., p. 32.
31. Ibid., p. 11.
32. "The Beloved Community," as cited at ibid., p. 17.
33. Ibid., p. 33.
34. Ibid., p. 19.
35. *A Religion for Greatness*, p. 45.
36. G. Louis Joughin and Edmund M. Morgan, *The Legacy of Sacco and Vanzetti* (New York: Harcourt Brace, 1948), p. 226.
37. *Worship and a Well Ordered Life*, p. 126.
38. Ibid., p. 174.
39. Ibid., pp. 160 ff.
40. *A Religion for Greatness*, p. 33.
41. *Worship and a Well Ordered Life*, p. 1.
42. *A Religion for Greatness*, p. 33.
43. Ibid., p. 21.
44. Ibid., p. 22.

Clarence Skinner:
Building a New Kind of Church

Carl Seaburg

I.

There are probably few among our two hundred thousand Unitarian Universalists who now recognize the name of Clarence Russell Skinner. If pressed, some may recollect that in the denominational buildings atop Beacon Hill in Boston, one is named Skinner House. They may not know for whom it is named, nor know that Skinner's photograph, which once hung proudly in its entrance hall, was shunted over to the staff lounge at 25 Beacon Street, the denominational headquarters. Efforts were made to have it returned to Skinner House, which after all was purchased with money from Skinner's widow, but nothing came of that. Now it has been banished to dwell in the dim obscurity of the portrait storage room [at least as of June 1994]. How are the mighty fallen!

More may recall that there is a modest program of Unitarian Universalist books published by an entity called Skinner House Press. Originally this venture was run from within Beacon Press. But early on it too was shipped over to the Unitarian Universalist Association's Publications Office.

And once each year, at General Assembly, an award is given for a sermon concerned with the social implications of religion. This award, which has been given since 1959, is named in honor of Clarence Skinner.

This lack of recognition should not be surprising. After all,

Skinner retired as dean of the Crane Theological School at Tufts in 1945—nearly half a century ago. He died four years later in 1949 at the relatively early age of sixty-eight, twelve years before the [Unitarian and Universalist] merger took place. Nearly all those who trained for our ministry under his leadership have now themselves retired from its active practice. Or joined him on the next stage of our eternal journey.

So it is well to begin this consideration of his achievements—and what meaning they have for us today—with a quick overview of his career. Let me spread before you a series of imaginary snapshots.[1]

The first one is a four-generation photograph including his great-grandfather Warren Skinner, a Universalist minister in Vermont, his grandfather Charles A. Skinner, a Universalist minister who served churches in Connecticut and the Boston area, his father Charles M. Skinner, editor of the newspaper the *Brooklyn Eagle*, and the young baby, Clarence Russell Skinner, born in 1881 in Brooklyn, New York. Because it is an imaginary photograph I can include his great-grandfather, who of course was dead by the time young Clarence was born. But it makes the point of how deeply-rooted his family was in Universalism and in its ministry.

The next photograph would be in 1900 showing the schoolboy, solemn and scholarly, as he graduated from Erasmus Hall High School in Brooklyn. It was not for nothing that his editor-father had read Homer and Plato to him and his brother Harold when they were young. Or regaled them with the plays of Shakespeare, challenged them with Emerson's essays, or exposed them to the ideas of Henry David Thoreau. Or made them acquainted with the poetry of Walt Whitman when many still considered that poet risqué or even lewd.

The third would show the youth at St. Lawrence University in Canton, New York. He graduated from St. Lawrence in 1904 after being prominent in dramatics, active on the debating team, editor of the college paper, and president of the graduating class while also earning his Phi Beta Kappa key. During his years at St. Lawrence he occasionally preached in the Canton Universalist Church.

The fourth photograph would show Skinner in one of his college acting roles. At first he hoped to become an actor. After all, an uncle was the famous Otis A. Skinner, a matinee idol of the Gay Nineties and as distinguished an actor as the four Barrymores put together. A daughter, Cornelia Otis Skinner, was Clarence's cousin, and herself became noted for her dramatic monologues and later her witty books. Both acting and the ministry seemed to be part of the Skinner heritage.

But the fifth photograph would reveal that the young man decided on the ministry and would show him in 1904 when he became assistant to Dr. Frank Oliver Hall, the distinguished minister of the Church of the Divine Paternity in New York City, now known as the Fourth Universalist Society. One of the guiding principles he learned from Dr. Hall was that "religion has to do with reality." While there he worked in the Settlement House the church had established on the east side, and at its Sunshine Farm.

The sixth photograph would have been taken on April 8, 1906, showing Skinner after he was ordained at Divine Paternity on Palm Sunday evening. Oddly enough, Skinner never graduated from a theological school, though he became dean of one.

The seventh photograph would be a wedding photograph taken on October 16, 1906. The bride was the former Clara Ayres of Stamford, Connecticut, whom he had met while at St. Lawrence.

The eighth photograph would show Skinner when he became minister of the Universalist Church in Mt. Vernon, New York, also in 1906. He served this parish, which was just above the Bronx, for five years until 1910. Skinner took the lead in getting them to build a new church. When he left, the parish had doubled in size.

While living out in the then-quiet suburb of Mt. Vernon, he did not neglect the problems of the inner city that he had become familiar with while at Divine Paternity. He still gave considerable time to working in the settlement houses in the slums of Manhattan.

It should be remembered that this was a period when the "Social Gospel" was much in the minds of thinking Christians. Walter Rauschenbusch, Professor of Church History at Rochester Theological Seminary, had published *Christianity and the Social Crisis* in 1907, and this book and articles by many others had stirred much discussion. How should social institutions be morally reorganized? How could public morality be brought to express Christian principles?

One of the ways Skinner did this, in addition to his work in the settlement houses, was to initiate a meeting of New York ministers of various denominations who were interested in the peace question. In time, this group formally organized and became the Church Peace Union. A staunch, unwavering pacifism became the core of Skinner's life.

The ninth photo would show Skinner in 1910 when he left Mt. Vernon and became minister of the Grace Universalist Church in Lowell, Massachusetts. This was a step up to a larger church, one of two Universalist churches in that community. While there he started the first church forum in New England. This met on Sunday evenings. Many outstanding leaders spoke from its platform to capacity crowds. Clara Skinner reported the hall often packed with 400 to 500 people. To show how progressive this forum was, Dr. W. E. B. DuBois was listed as one of the speakers in January 1914. Skinner's purpose in the forum was, he stated, to try to bring the world into the church and to carry the church out into the world. The format of the forum, which would later be copied at the Community Church of Boston, began with a short worship service, had an offering to meet their expenses, then listened to the speaker, followed by a free questioning period.

My last photograph would show Clarence Skinner meeting Dr. Lee McCollester, Dean of Crane Theological School at Tufts College. McCollester was greatly impressed by this earnest young minister and asked him to come to Tufts and teach the subject of Applied Christianity. So, in 1914, he moved his energies and his ideals to the campus in Medford.[2]

You now have—flipping through these ten imaginary photographs—a quick picture of the life of young Skinner. Long steeped in Universalist faith, tutored in the social problems of the day, active in developing solutions for the problems he was encountering, he at last had a pulpit from which he could affect a significant group of people—the future leaders of his beloved denomination.

It is my argument in this essay that the principal aim throughout Skinner's life was to rethink, restructure, revivify the Universalist church he had inherited, and to transform it into a church which could more effectively serve the twentieth century.

There is no document that says this was his intent or guiding principle. But I think it is an accurate inference from a study of his whole life.

There was a deep strain of mysticism in Skinner, and he later expressed his goal in a poetic fashion:

Why worship half-truths? Why give your highest loyalties to atoms? These are the broken arcs. Ascend the mountain of vision and see that humanity is one, wealth is one, truth, justice are one. Let us have done with lesser things and join in a common, universal life, whose tides flow through our souls.[3]

So it is my aim in this essay to evaluate Skinner's goals and contributions to our Unitarian Universalist faith, and to show how what he did in his time can still give us direction and inspiration for our lives.

II.

Skinner grew up in a rationalistic, optimistic, progressive faith that probably seemed permanent to him as a young man. But the brutalities of the twentieth century—the sufferings he had seen in the tenements of New York, the enormous horrors of the First World War, then the severity of the Great Depression—shattered any kind of a superficial Pollyanna-ish faith.

However, Skinner did not give up hope. Some of his contemporaries became pessimistic and abandoned all their hopeful dreams. They turned to fascist or communistic or Calvinistic solutions.

Not Skinner. Where did hope lie? His answer was in the liberal churches. Liberals, of course, are the eternal scapegoats. Nobody follows their suggestions, yet when conservative plans go awry—as they always do—who gets blamed? The liberals, naturally!

My argument is simple: that Skinner very early on saw the need to rethink religious liberalism, specifically Universalism, in the light of the social problems of the twentieth century. He did this first for himself in the graduate courses he took at Columbia and Harvard, and what he learned from his courses at the Boston School of Social Workers.

He brought this thinking into his church work and into the work he did in New York in the settlement houses and in helping to form the Church Peace Union.

Within the denomination he had been appointed secretary to its Social Service Commission as early as 1910. He then wrote a series of articles which were published in the denominational journal, the *Christian Leader*, and were subsequently revised into a book called *The Social Implications of Universalism*. He was instrumental in the denomination's adoption of "A Declaration of Social Principles" in 1917.

In the midst of the First World War this contained a statement Skinner fully supported saying that "War is brutalizing, wasteful, and ineffective. We therefore pledge ourselves to work for the organization and federation of the world, that peace may be secured at the earliest possible date consistent with justice for all." For many years he had been a convinced pacifist, aided in part by his Quaker mother's hatred of war. His stalwart defense of this position during the First World War earned him the ill-will of many on the Tufts campus.

My proposition is that he transferred his endeavors to radicalize the Universalism of the day to ever larger spheres of action. First he had worked directly in the slums and in the churches he was serving. Then he worked within the denomination. The call to Tufts gave him the opportunity to work with the oncoming generation of students who would become leaders and shapers in the denomination. Then in 1920 came his most important effort in this area: the creation of the Community Church of Boston.[4]

In 1931 the Macmillan Company published a book of sermons edited by Skinner, that had been preached at the Community Church. In his introduction to this collection, which he edited, he states his goal quite clearly.

First he comments on the negative criticism by many of the church of that period at the end of the First World War. He was thinking, of course, of all the Christian churches. Critics, he wrote, have called the church "hopelessly out of date in its form of organization, unsound in its point of view, superfluous in modern civilization, and ineffective in its activities." Some of us might feel this is still true today.[5]

As he saw it there were four ways one could react to such criticism:

1. It is deserved, and therefore people should abandon the institution as hopeless.
2. The criticism is undeserved, and should be ignored.
3. One could plod on making minor adjustments and re-forms.
4. OR—and here I quote him: "One may set his hand to the task of building a new kind of church adapted to the new

age, thus creating a demonstration center that will prove what can be done by a radical reconstruction."[6]

This is what he attempted in organizing the Community Church of Boston. It was to be a "demonstration center" that would show what could be done by "a radical reconstruction" of the nature of a church. When he wrote "radical" that was what he meant, no merely shallow paint job to make the old facade seem new.

Let me give you a summary of his "new kind of a church" in a short history of the Community Church of Boston from 1920 to 1936, the years during which he was its leader.

In 1919 Skinner gathered together about thirty people who had become acquainted through their active participation in social reform work. They were men and women not satisfied with the conventional churches of the day. Yet they felt the need for a spiritual and religious motivation to help them as they tried to build a new social order out of the wreckage left by the First World War.

They consulted with John Haynes Holmes, who had recently transformed his Unitarian Church of the Messiah in New York City into a Community Church. Skinner had known Holmes since Holmes arrived in New York in February, 1907. Sharing many similar ideas their friendship continued, even after Skinner left the New York area.

Skinner had been impressed by the recent actions Holmes had taken in New York City. When Jenkins Lloyd Jones died in the fall of 1918, the Abraham Lincoln Centre in Chicago, whose director he had been, asked Holmes if he would take Jones's place. Holmes was greatly drawn to this offer. He had been almost twelve years in New York, and while his large congregation loved him, gave him a free pulpit, accepted his pacifism during the hysteria of the First World War years, and provided him with an adequate staff, the great liberating tradition of Jones and the centrality of Chicago were enormous attractions.

At an overflow congregational meeting on December 30, 1918, Holmes described to his members the Chicago offer and its attraction to him. However, he said he would stay in New York, if they would agree to certain propositions which would make their church non-denominational, change its name, and establish membership on an open basis. The congregation agreed, Holmes stayed, and so the Community Church of New York was born.

Skinner had been following these developments closely. He resonated to Holmes's ringing statement that

> [t]he Community Church is the logical completion and perfection of the liberal movement in modern religion. It accomplishes boldly what Liberalism has been attempting timidly, in that it finally (1) shifts the basis of religion from God to man; (2) moves from the individual to the social group as the center of religious life; and (3) accepts the community in place of the denomination as the unit of spiritual integration.[7]

If Holmes was the primary inspiration for Skinner, there was a second example less well-known. This was the "Sunday Commons" run by Rabbi Charles Fleischer. He had come to Boston in 1894 to be the rabbi of Temple Israel. On his arrival in Boston he was met at the railway station by the great Unitarian pastor Edward Everett Hale, who put his arms around his shoulders and said: "Now, my son, you, too, are one of the preachers of New England."

Fleischer served Temple Israel until 1911, when he resigned and formed the "Sunday Commons." His reason was that his "positions on radicalism and universalism are more pronounced than my congregation seems ready to accept." Indeed, he was considered one of the most intellectual and radical rabbis in America, outspoken on a variety of topics including marriage, divorce, religion, labor, literature, evolution, and opposition to capital punishment.

The "Sunday Commons" was a non-sectarian religious movement, designed to interpret American life through a series of forum speakers. It lasted until sometime after the war. In 1922 Fleischer went to New York to become a newspaper editor and radio commentator. When he left, he suggested that his followers attend Skinner's Community Church. Many did.[8]

By October 1919 Skinner's group was drawing up its plans to form a Community Church in Boston similar to Holmes's church in New York. However, they were going to begin on an even more daring basis. They would not create their church from an already thriving church with a large congregation and a proven people-attracting minister. Essentially, they would begin *de novo*, from scratch as it were.

They held their first meeting on January 11, 1920, in a rented hall instead of a church building, because they did not want those who might attend to think that this was just another conventional ordinary church meeting. Nearly three hundred people attended the first meeting in Steinert Hall! Not only had they publicized it well among their various groups of friends and associates, they apparently had struck something in the public mood of the time. A period after the horrors of the First World War, with all its intensive disruptions, when people were looking for new and better ways to shape their living and their society.

One must remember the time period in which they began their enterprise. Radio was still in its infancy in 1920, the factories of Detroit were just beginning to mass produce cheap automobiles, road travel was still pretty primitive, motion pictures were still silent, seven years would pass before Lindbergh soloed the Atlantic, and television was thirty years in the future. So the kind of things which keep people from church today were not really operative seventy-five years ago.

Succeeding Sunday meetings were equally well supported, attendance varying somewhat with the speakers and topics that were chosen. Because of this "cordial response"—as Skinner phrased it—a permanent organization, "The Community

Church of Boston," was formed that October. Incorporation took place on April 12, 1922.

After four years of meeting in the Steinert Hall on Boylston Street, the group took the step of moving into a theater in order to accommodate the increasing numbers attending. They rented the Copley Theater which could seat 1,000 people, double the capacity of Steinert Hall. The larger space attracted more people and "the nucleus of loyal members" who did the ongoing work of the organization, "grew rapidly."[9]

Who was attracted to this new kind of a church? The monthly preaching visits of Holmes drew "a wide assortment of pacifists and social radicals."[10] Skinner describes the other attenders:

> People of all types came to the services—rich and poor, black and white, Jew and Gentile, educated and illiterate. The contrast between the congregation of this church and that of the older sectarian churches was perhaps greater than the contrast between the pulpits, although that was important and striking.[11]

Many a UU church of the 1990s would be happy if its congregation was composed of such a varied group. Even with our "Welcoming Congregations" program, we have a difficult time attracting such a diverse mix of people.

After seven years, the new congregation took a bold step and moved their services into Symphony Hall in Boston. As Skinner notes, this was a "breath-taking adventure" because Symphony Hall had a seating capacity of 2,600 people. "However," he adds, "the membership took counsel of their courage rather than their fears and made the move!"[12]

What was the result? Eighteen hundred people attended that first service on October 3, 1926. We have no church in the UUA today that can boast such a turnout. "The attendance," Skinner wrote in 1931, continued on "a very large scale, sometimes above and sometimes below that of the first day.

On rare occasions the hall has been filled to standing capacity, but the average has remained well above 1,200."[13] During 1935, the average attendance reached 1,500.

III.

What was new about this kind of church that attracted so many people consistently? Let us look at the areas of the pulpit, worship, and social service.

From the beginning, there was a different conception of the leadership of the church. They did not have a called minister. Skinner explicitly preferred to function simply as the "leader." Since he had a full-time position at the Tufts College School of Religion as it was then called, he limited himself to conducting the Sunday service, chairing the board, giving general oversight, and occasionally being the Sunday speaker. He also performed weddings, funerals, and did counseling. It was hardly part-time work.

A testimony to Skinner's effectiveness as a speaker was given by one member of Community Church. Carl Anthonsen wrote the following in his diary under the date of Sunday, January 6, 1929:

> Another interesting session at C.C. John Haynes Holmes, who is leaving for Palestine, and Clarence Skinner spoke on "Religious Experience in the Modern Age." I found Mr. Skinner the more interesting. While I have heard him often as chairman of a meeting, this was the first time I heard him speak his own opinions. He delivered a fiery speech in which he handled fundamentalism without gloves. In a sweeping indictment he said that orthodox clergymen say things to each other that they do not dare to say to their flocks. The Community Church, he said, is the beginning of a new chapter in spiritual history. Incidentally, the C.C. is celebrating its 9th anniversary this month.[14]

What Skinner envisioned for this new kind of a church they were creating was a community pulpit, composed of a collective of specialists, or as he once phrased it, drawing on his college experience, "a faculty of ministers." Each would have "distinctive qualities to contribute to the services."

The people chosen as Sunday speakers came from every branch of the religious spectrum, and were chosen whether they were ministers or not. Holmes would comment on their twentieth anniversary, "The result is a ministry of well-nigh unparalleled variety and power. I know of nothing to compare with it excepting pulpits maintained in much the same spirit by certain of the great universities of the country. . . . We have here a program of prophecy which is as effective as it is novel."[15]

Let me list a few of names of the people who spoke during Skinner's tenure: Norman Thomas, Earl Browder, Margaret Sanger, Dorothy Thompson, Scott Nearing, Will Durant, Stephen Wise, William Ernest Hocking, Krishnamurti, Maude Royden, Bertrand Russell, Reinhold Niebuhr, Eva Le Gallienne, James Weldon Johnson, Walter White, W. E. B. DuBois, Samuel Eliot Morison, and even James Michael Curley!

In addition, Skinner, drawing upon his community forum experience in Lowell, began the custom of having an open forum after the church service in which members of the congregation could ask questions of the morning speaker and discuss the topic of the day. His wife remarked that Skinner really "sparkled" (her word) during the question and answer period!

Today we might call this "the sermon talkback," and while for a time that was fairly common in some of our churches, it seems mostly to have died away again. But this was done every Sunday at Community Church from 1920 until today. When such practices become common or even "old hat," we forget who pioneered them. Skinner did, in Boston, where he was demonstrating the building of a "new kind of church."

And such an idea aroused opposition at first from some

who felt it took away from the atmosphere of reverence and worship. But the Community Church congregation made ample opportunity for people to withdraw from the service, before they began the discussion period.

Next, consider the form of worship in Community Church. Remember, we are looking back nearly three-quarters of a century to practices which now are so common to us, we may not realize how startling they were to the people of the 1920s when they were first introduced by Skinner.

In a 1939 collection of papers by the faculty at the School of Religion at Tufts, Skinner had this to say about what religion meant to him. (Please note that I have degenderized it as I feel sure he would do today):

> To me, the highest type of religious experience is that which gives people a sense of unity and universality. Most of our life is spent in narrow segments. Our horizon is hemmed in by kitchen walls, office desks, narrow prejudices of race, class, or creed. In religion, these partialisms, broken fragments of life, are lifted into a vast and profound oneness. Our littleness becomes stretched to cosmic greatness. Elemental forces roll through our beings, sensitize our perceiving, and quicken our lives.[16]

The feeling of Skinner and the congregation at Community Church was that their practice of worship closely followed the original pattern of colonial New England churches. The service was very simple, no liturgy or ritual. They did differ from the Puritans in having music as an important part of the service.

But like the Puritans they placed great importance on the sermon, it was not a short, polite, pleasant fifteen-minute essay as it had become in the churches of the 1920s. It was frequently of an hour's duration, and required genuine intellectual effort on the part of the hearers.

Skinner made a serious effort to revise and modernize the whole format of the worship service for Community Church. The invocation each Sunday was not the repetition of a string of Bible verses, as was common then, but written anew for each service. "Its object," said Skinner, "was to state simply and clearly in non-mystical language the purpose of the coming together of the people."[17]

He gave one example in his 1931 book, which I would like to repeat for you. You will not be struck by it, because the tone has become that of most of our Unitarian Universalist ministers today. But for its time it was startling, and indeed one can say, revolutionary.

> We come to this service to invoke the mood of reverence and worship: to lift our thoughts in aspiration toward all high and holy aims: to renew our loyalty to the good, the true, and the beautiful: and to consecrate ourselves again to common service to the common good.[18]

Skinner made every effort to rethink all the elements of the worship service. Here is what he said about hymns:

> The hymns avoid so far as possible the old ecclesiastical terminology. . . . Wherever possible, new verses are sung to old music, as for instance the popular "Onward Christian Soldiers" is transformed into the modern and stirring words of "Forward Through the Ages."[19]

Frederick Lucian Hosmer wrote this hymn in 1908, but the first Unitarian Universalist hymnbook to use it was the *Beacon Song and Service Book* of 1935. They had already been singing it at Community Church for over a decade.

There were several people in the congregation who contributed occasional hymn revisions, and they made much use of hymns written by John Haynes Holmes. Some of the old hymns written by [John Greenleaf] Whittier and Samuel Longfellow were kept, "but a vigorous attempt is made to eliminate such antiquated sentiments as jar on the sensibilities of modern minds." As Skinner added, "There is no capitulation in the attempt to make our emotions intellectually respectable."[20]

Skinner admitted that they had not solved the problem of having a choir, but they made regular use of the wonderful organ in Symphony Hall and also frequently had a string quartet. On occasion they would have Jewish or African-American soloists.

In the matter of Scripture readings, Skinner broke with the old tradition, still common in those years, of having the first reading taken from the Old Testament, and the second reading from the New Testament. Some churches were experimenting even then with taking one reading from the Bible and a second one from a modern source. But Skinner felt that "no ecclesiastical authority or sanction is necessary for a reading which lifts the spirit, catches fire in people's hearts, and reveals some noble reach of the imagination." So in choosing their readings they drew—as we now commonly do today—on the whole range of writings of those "who have voiced the high hopes and common aspirations of humanity."[21]

Prayer, Skinner admitted, was the most baffling of the elements of the service in a thoroughly modernized church. No church, he felt, could dodge the question of prayer: either continue the practice through conviction, or modify it to harmonize with the modern world, or abandon it all together.

Skinner felt something analogous to prayer had to be kept if there was to be a complete and effective service of worship. "There must be," he wrote, "some outpouring of the soul, some lift of spirit in a church if it is to be differentiated from the lecture platform." He borrowed and adapted a phrase from Ruskin to say that prayer was an "escape into the infinite."[22]

The prayer, he maintained, should be "an opening toward the universal." But in any case should fulfill the task of relating humans to the largest dimensions of life, what some might want to call God and others the Source of Life or the Creative Spirit. Again, he gives an example, but I refrain from quoting it, because it is similar to what you might hear in a UU church today, but would not have heard in either a Unitarian or Universalist church in the 1920s except at Boston's Community Church.

Not every one who attended a Community Church service came there to worship. Many came to hear the speaker and to take part in the forum which followed. Often their behavior during the preceding service was most casual. I can remember once attending a Community Church service at Symphony Hall, perhaps about 1942, and seeing one member of the congregation busily reading a newspaper while the worship service went on. He only put it away when the speaker of the day began. But then I have within the past year attended worship services where a few UU ministers came in with cups of coffee from which they drank during the service.

Finally, I would like to take a look at the social service side of this church. Social problems and social ethics were always important to Skinner and he taught courses on both those subjects when I was at Crane. The area of social action was a vital part of a church's life to him.

In the early years, the chief social justice work of the Church was focused on the Sacco-Vanzetti case. This was a case in which two Italian immigrants and anarchists were arrested for an armed robbery and murder. In a trial marked with tainted evidence and stained by prejudice against the defendants because of their ethnic background and their beliefs, they were condemned to death. A long legal battle between their condemnation in 1921 and their execution in 1927 then took place.

The Community Church became interested in their case "from the beginning, holding a meeting three months after the trial at which . . . some of the witnesses spoke."[23] It worked hard to inform the public of the miscarriage of justice which they felt was happening. Skinner and his wife attended a number of the trial sessions. He later wrote a clear and forceful account of the trial. Many other American notables joined the cause, but in spite of the most intense efforts, [Massachusetts] Governor Alvan T. Fuller would not grant clemency and let the execution of the two men take place.

In 1978, the Commonwealth of Massachusetts pardoned the two victims, but oddly enough that didn't bring them back to life. As John Haynes Holmes said in his twentieth-anniversary sermon, The Community Church's work "in the Sacco-Vanzetti case was a model of what a church may do when confronted by a wrong which has its origin in the pride, power, and prejudice of the chosen classes of the community."[24]

Another instance of the church's dedication to social causes came when it attempted to hire a hotel hall so that Margaret Sanger, the pioneer birth control advocate, could present her case for changing the laws of Massachusetts to allow this practice. By indirect means the city of Boston prevented the hall's use, thus denying her the right of free speech on a public matter. Incensed, Skinner invited her to preach on the subject at a Sunday morning service. As he said in introducing her, "The officials of the City of Boston do not dare or care to disturb this religious service."[25] He challenged the mayor or the police chief to interfere, but they did not and the meeting was held. This was the first public hearing for this view in Boston, which now is law. It is easy to forget the people who pioneer our freedoms.

A Social Justice Committee was also formed in the church and among its other campaigns in the Skinner years it worked to free the Scottsboro boys from the false charges of rape which had been leveled against them, it sent food, clothing, and medical supplies to the Spanish democracy in its struggle against Franco, and worked for the rights of seamen, and against capital punishment.

But this is not all. As Holmes said, the Community Church

"fought poverty. . . . It has defended civil liberties. . . . It has espoused the cause of prison reform. . . . It has assailed militarism, political corruption, economic exploitation, racial discrimination, and religious bigotry. It has remembered always the Negro, the unemployed, the workers. . . . It has sought only to save the people through the application of social justice to the common life."[26] In all these areas of need, it was reflecting the concerns of Clarence Skinner.

How to assess what the Community Church accomplished while Skinner was its leader? It certainly provided an opening for much progressive thought to be heard and debated. It did reach, Sunday after Sunday, more than a thousand intelligent, concerned citizens. It pioneered a number of useful social causes and upheld liberal ideals.

In its statement of purpose it advocated three principles which I feel are still valid for our congregations today. These were that a congregation should be a free fellowship of men and women united

1. for the study of universal religion,
2. seeking to apply ethical ideals to individual life, and
3. seeking to apply the co-operative principle to all forms of social and economic life.[27]

When Holmes came to Boston in 1962 to help in the dedication of Skinner House, whose purchase had been made possible by a generous contribution from his widow, Clara Skinner, and to assist in the hanging of his photograph in the house named in his honor, he summed up in these words, Skinner's great contribution:

These were days which saw him at the zenith of his power—faithful to his service of the Universalists, but reaching out more and more now to the lofty extension of the greater cause of the Community Church. This church, moved and directed by Skinner's devoted leadership, pointed the way to the Church Universal and fulfilled in large and potent measure the secular idealism of a new and greater church. There were mighty deeds in those days which began the transformation of organized religion, both orthodox and liberal, and Skinner led the van.[28]

Even when we strain the hyperbole of rhetoric out of this statement, we can find the conclusion towards which I have been reaching—that once Skinner came into the active ministry, all his efforts were directed toward reshaping the old-fashioned Universalist church of the day as he knew it, into something which captured the essential spirit of Universalism—but poured that old vintage wine into a dramatically different new bottle.

Whether you look at his work at Mt. Vernon, New York, or Lowell, Massachusetts, or consider the pioneering work he did for the denomination's Declaration of Social Principles, or take into account the social ethic courses he taught at Tufts, and the lasting effect he had on the principles of his many students at the Theological School, and principally the work he did with the Community Church in Boston, he was faithful to his central idea of building a new kind of church that could be a model to all other churches.[29]

IV.

What effect did Skinner's demonstration church have on the Unitarian Universalist movement? If we look at the area of the pulpit, we would say not much. Partly this is because few churches could afford the cost of such a great variety of speakers. The Germantown, Pennsylvania, church tried using the smorgasbord of speakers approach for about forty years from 1936, but have shifted back to the common practice or regular preaching by the settled minister.

As to worship, I think we only need look at the latest UUA hymnbook, *Singing the Living Tradition*. This strikes me as exactly the kind of hymnal that Skinner was working toward in his innovations at Community Church. He was doing it in the 1920s, and this book did not become available until 1993. But that's the definition of pioneers, that they are ahead of their time. Certainly in his lectures at Tufts when I was there, Skinner was pushing us toward the concepts he was embodying at Community Church. I can only think that he was one of the forces moving us toward more genuine worship experiences.

In the field of social service, his courses at Tufts on social problems and social ethics were specific and detailed, and represented a lifelong commitment. He certainly instilled in many of his students a deep impulse toward social service as an essential part of the life of the church. It was only at the end of his life that the Universalist Service Committee was organized, but the work that it did, and its successor, the Unitarian Universalist Service Committee, were close to his heart. And he was particularly concerned that individual churches work on their own local concerns, too.

What was important about Skinner, in my view, was not that he was a brilliant scholar. He was not Liberalism's Reinhold Niebuhr or Karl Barth. Though he was well-educated and wide-ranging, he was not our John Dewey. I can remember as a student being surprised when he mispronounced several words of which I knew the "proper" pronunciation. I found this rather encouraging—that you could be very intelligent and still not perfect.

What I do know is that in the class notes I took in his courses, I had my first serious exposure to the social problems of our contemporary society. Skinner went into them in great detail. And year by year, this knowledge was imparted to the students who took his courses, and reached out to affect our congregations, and the people in them, and the people attracted to them.

It was not even important that Skinner should have well-thought-out views on evolutionism, individualism, or psychology. Or a fully-developed liberal theology. James Hunt's essay on his liberal theology points out that he did not.

Skinner's mystical approach to religion was valuable, and has not been adequately studied. There are weaknesses in it. He was nowhere near as quotable as Emerson. But it is a dimension of liberal religion which often gets ignored and overlooked. There are even people who think we are not mystical at all. I think that is an error. I feel there is a deep mystical strain under the surface in Unitarian Universalism and we ignore it at our loss.

What Hunt did find important was that Skinner "never ceased to insist that the power of religion was located in its universal vision," or that "universalism had social implications," and "affirmed the creative uses of the contemporary and called for the restructuring of thought, of worship, and of the church in terms of present needs and opportunities."

I am not advocating that we should recreate the Community Church of Boston in our setting. Holmes thought, for instance, that the Community Church would be "the church of the future." In that he has been—so far—shown wrong, but what Skinner was doing for his time—and challenging us to do in our time—is to continually reshape the churches that we inherit—whether as ministers or lay people—so that they can face up to the new challenges and opportunities of the days that lie ahead.

We ourselves have not reached the end of the evolution of the idea of the church. We must continue the kind of work that Skinner made central to his life ministry—always building a new kind of church. Always reaching out for a vision of the church that lies just beyond our grasp but which with hard, dedicated work can be conjured into being.

We need in our time to do the same kind of pioneering work that Skinner undertook in the first half of this century: the rethinking of religious liberalism for the twenty-first century. We need to put our impress on religious liberalism for the next one hundred years, as Skinner did for his time.[30]

Notes

1. For information on Skinner's life, the most succinct source is Russell E. Miller, *The Larger Hope* (Boston: Unitarian Universalist Association, 1985), Vol. 2, especially pp. 496-500, and footnotes for Chapter 26. See pp. 709-711. A typo is the dating of Skinner's ordination in 1905; it was 1906. For a personal view, see Alfred Storer Cole, *Clarence Skinner, Prophet of Twentieth Century Universalism* (Boston: Universalist Historical Society, 1956). A fairly complete biography of Skinner will be found in Charles A. Gaines, "Clarence R. Skinner: Image of a Movement" (unpublished special BD thesis, Crane Theological School, Tufts University, 1961, now at the Harvard Divinity School library archives). This account of Skinner's life is particularly valuable for the interviews with Clara Skinner and others. Gaines also thoughtfully deposited his interview notes at Harvard. It is helpful that the first chapter of this present book is an updating of this biography by Charles Howe, done with the approval of Charles Gaines.

2. The Universalist Historical Society *Journal* (Vol. V, 1964-65) has a fairly complete bibliography of Skinner's writings (pp. 65-77) by Alan Seaburg, now updated and reprinted in this volume. Volume III (1962) of the *Journal* has an extract from the Gaines thesis, "Clarence R. Skinner: The Dark Years," pp. 1-13. Volume VII (1967-68) of the *Journal* has an article by James D. Hunt, "The Liberal Theology of Clarence R. Skinner" (pp. 102-120). This serious critical study emphasizes both Skinner's weaknesses and strengths. See especially pp. 119-120. It too is reprinted in this volume.

3. From an unpublished manuscript by Skinner, "Religious Insights into the Unities and Universalists," as quoted by Alfred S. Cole in "Clarence R. Skinner, Prophet of the Larger Faith," *The Universalist Leader*, April 1961, p. 76.

4. In his early years at Tufts, Skinner took on the pastorate of the Medford Hillside Universalist Church, one of two Universalist

churches in the city. He started there in 1917 and planned to use it as a working laboratory for the theological students. His ministry was a success, with congregations increasing and a parish house built, but the reputation he gained for his opposition to the war was one of the reasons he left the church in 1919. See Gaines, "Clarence R. Skinner: Image of a Movement," p. 72.

5. This, and subsequent descriptions of how the Community Church in Boston operated, is taken from Clarence R. Skinner, editor, *A Free Pulpit in Action* (New York: The Macmillan Co., 1931), pp. 1-17. Particularly valuable in this collection of talks is that a stenographic account of the forum questions and answers is printed after nearly all the addresses. For an interesting sample see the talk on birth control by Margaret Sanger, James Landis, and Clarence Skinner, pp. 164-185. Cynthia Foster (a member of Community Church) has furnished me with a list of the dates on which these addresses were given, which I have deposited in the archives at Harvard Divinity School.

6. Ibid., p. 1.

7. John Haynes Holmes saw the Community Church as one that would not be denominationally oriented, but community oriented. His definitive work on the movement is his *New Churches For Old* (New York: Dodd, Mead & Co., 1922). See especially Chapters 8 and 9 on the principles, organization, message, and work of the Community Church. Carl Hermann Voss, in *Rabbi and Minister* (Cleveland: World Publishing, 1964), tells of changing the Church of the Messiah into the New York Community Church on pp. 154-158, and the story of the founding of Boston's Community Church on pp. 174-175. Also helpful in this recounting is "Three Score and Ten Years," a sermon preached by Bruce Southworth on January 29, 1989, celebrating the seventieth anniversary of the Community Church of New York.

Holmes's church did not operate exactly as the Boston church did. In New York the forum did not follow the morning service but was held Sunday evenings. Also, Holmes preached every Sunday except the first Sunday of the month, which he reserved for Boston's Community Church. He gave his services to the Boston church asking for only his expenses.

In a note written for the "Community Church News" in January 1940, Skinner mentions a third factor in launching the

Boston Community Church: "At this time, a series of articles was written by Mr. [Joseph Ernest] Macafee of New York, outlining the possibilities of a radical reorganization of church forces. He pointed out the failures, or at least, weaknesses of sectarianism, and looked forward to the community principle as the reorganizing force."

8. Information on Fleischer came from Cynthia Foster, whose sisters, Virginia Anderson and the late Dorothy Wilder, attended the "Sunday Commons," until Fleischer's departure for New York, when they switched to the Community Church. Fleischer's meetings were held at 30 Huntington Avenue, said Mrs. Anderson. Additional information comes from his obituaries in the Boston *Herald* and the Boston *Post,* July 3, 1942. See also Arthur Mann, "Charles Fleischer's Religion of Democracy," *Commentary*, XVII, June 1954, pp. 557-565.

9. Skinner, *A Free Pulpit*, pp. 2-3.

10. Voss, *Rabbi and Minister*, p. 274.

11. Skinner, *A Free Pulpit*, pp. 3-4.

12. Ibid., p. 4.

13. Ibid.

14. Carl Anthonsen, diary entry, January 6, 1929 (supplied by his widow Cynthia Foster).

15. John Haynes Holmes, twentieth-anniversary sermon, January 7, 1940, from Community Church archives.

16. *Tufts Papers on Religion*, 1939, pp. 12-13.

17. Skinner, *A Free Pulpit*, p. 10.

18. Ibid.

19. Ibid.

20. Ibid., pp. 10-11.

21. Ibid., p. 12.

22. Ibid., pp. 13-14.

23. *1939 History and Principles* (Boston: The Community Church of Boston, 1939), p. 8.

24. Ibid., p. 9.

25. Skinner, *A Free Pulpit*, p. 167.

26. Holmes, January 7, 1940, sermon, p. 9.

27. Gaines, "Clarence R. Skinner: Image of a Movement," p. 82.

28. John Haynes Holmes, 1962 letter, Harvard Divinity School archives.

29. I have described the Community Church during the period of Skinner's ministry from 1920 to 1936. He envisioned it, among other things, as a demonstration church that would set an example for other congregations. In many ways it was successful in doing this. From January 1920 until May 1924 it met in Steinert Hall. From October 1924 until May 1926 it met in the Copley Theater. Part of the discomfort with the Copley Theater was that rather peculiar stage sets sometimes formed the backdrop for the services. From October 1926 until May 1942 meetings were held in Symphony Hall.

Skinner was succeeded by Donald Lothrop, who served from 1936 to 1974. During this period the church moved from Symphony Hall into the nearby, but smaller, Jordan Hall (October 1942 to May 1949). From there it went to John Hancock Hall (October 1949 to May 1953). An invitation to Owen Lattimore to speak caused the John Hancock Insurance Company (hardly in the radical spirit of its namesake!) to deny the use of the hall to Community Church, which then shifted its services to the auditorium of the Boston Conservatory of Music (October 1953 to May 1968). This was quite some distance from where the religious education classes were being held in Copley Square in the five-story United Service Organization building which they had bought in 1946 for headquarters. Services then moved into the nearby New England Life Hall (October 1969 to May 1974). But again, a speaker who had been to Castro's Cuba attracted picketers who invaded the service with stink bombs. The church was asked to move again and went to Boston University's Morse Auditorium, formerly Temple Israel (October 1974 to May 1987). Donald Lothrop retired in 1974 and was succeeded by Philip Zwerling, who served until 1978. Following him came William Alberts, who served until 1991. Jack Mendelsohn did an interim ministry until 1993, and was succeeded by Tim Anderson. Anderson left in 1996 and David Olson is now leading the services.

During the McCarthy era, when the church was falsely attacked as being Communist, many members left the church, a significant setback from which the church has never fully recovered. During Alberts's ministry, the church refurbished its second floor area, named it Lothrop Hall, and its meetings have been held there since May 1987.

[The 1997 UUA Directory lists the church's certified membership at 84 with 61 contributing units and a budget of $150,000.]

It has continued its social service work and during Alberts's ministry became the first church in the Boston area to offer sanctuary to a Central American refugee whom it hosted for four years.

30. I would like to thank the following people for their great help in preparing this paper: Cynthia Foster, who has been a member of Community Church of Boston since 1924, for many items and particularly the quotation from her first husband's diary, the Carl Anthonsen entry for January 6, 1929; Donald Lothrop, minister emeritus of Community Church; Caroline Adams, office manager of Community Church; Bruce Southworth, minister of New York's Community Church; William J. Gardiner; Eugene Adams; Carolyn Kemmet, formerly of the Unitarian Universalist Association archives; and especially Alan Seaburg, former Curator of Manuscripts, Harvard Divinity School Library. I am also particularly indebted to the work of Charles Gaines in his biography of Skinner.

Selected Writings of
Clarence R. Skinner

❖

EDITED AND ANNOTATED BY JAMES D. HUNT

To let Clarence Skinner speak, I have included whole essays or whole chapters of his writings, rather than attempting to identify his themes and interests through a collage of brief quotations. These writings show both his youthful exuberance and his mature reflections. This section begins with a chapter from his first book, *The Social Implications of Universalism* (1915), and a news report of a provocative address to the Universalist ministers as he became dean of Crane Theological School in 1933.

Also included are thoughtful essays and addresses from Skinner's later years. These selections show his efforts to reformulate Universalist theology as universal religion. They represent his conception of religion, the role of religion in the university, his concept of the "unities and universals," and the relation of religion and science. The section concludes with an undated article, "What Is Worship?"

Skinner's last book, *A Religion for Greatness* (1945), like his first, together with his experiments in worship practices and church structure at the Community Church of Boston, had a significant effect on Universalist thought and practice.

The Social Implications of Universalism *grew out of a series of essays in* The Universalist Leader *in February and March 1915. This was Skinner's first year of teaching at the Crane Theological School; these selections might be viewed as an extended inaugural address. The chapters provide a comprehensive statement of his religious social philosophy and foreshadow much of his work, later seen most clearly in the Community Church of Boston. This little book became a Universalist classic and was revised and reissued in 1939.*

Skinner was writing in a time of hope in politics and the churches, as the impact of World War I had not yet influenced American theology. The more liberal denominations were adopting "social creeds" addressing the ills of the cities, the economic system, and poverty.

In Chapter 3, "God and Democracy," Skinner viewed Universalism as the purification of Christianity, stressing ethics more than theology and personal salvation, but already he was envisioning Universalism as a religion of universals that transcend all particular forms and parochial interests.—JDH

God and Democracy

All great social problems involve theological conceptions. We may divorce church from state, but we cannot separate the idea of God from the political life of the people. So intimate is the connection between religious and social development, that the history of tribal and national evolution reveals the fact that a particular type of theology is an almost inevitable concomitant of a particular type of society. There is a constant interaction between ideals of economic and political life on the one hand, and ideals of God on the other. As man attains increasing democracy, he conceives God as being more universal, more just and more intimately associated with life; and as God is conceived to be more universal, just and intimate, the idea begets more democracy among men. Social action and theological reaction are equal, and in the same direction.

In the olden times God was conceived to be aristocratic, imperious, partial, because the people were so; and the commonly accepted notions of deity never rise higher than the common social experience. Our religious terminology and imagery smack of imperialism and aristocracy. Therefore we find the old sacred literatures full of such statements as this, which in the Bhagavadgita is attributed to the Creator: "The fourfold division of castes was created by me according to the apportionment of qualities and duties." God is here imagined as dividing his human creatures into four distinct classes, each with appropriate powers. This supposed fiat of a partial deity became the constitution for the caste system of social, political and economic life which has held sway so universally and so imperiously among the peoples of the Orient. A caste system created a caste God and a caste God spread its sanction over a divisive and aristocratic society. Government used the church as a reinforcement for the execution of its tyrannies.

The Old Testament record of the dramatic struggle between the worshipers of Yaweh and Baal is illustrative of the clash between a democratic people with a democratic idea of God and an aristocratic people with an exploiting God. Prof. Lewis Wallis, author of "The Sociological Aspects of the Bible," has ingeniously but clearly shown the deep economic and political significance of this struggle. The Israelites were born to the rugged freedom of the hill country, inheritors of a rich social idealism, worshipers of a God, Yaweh, who stood for justice. The Amorites were a commercial people, with traditions of a slave class, worshipers, therefore, of Baal, who became the shekel raised to the *nth* power, a God who condoned greed and injustice. Professor Wallis therefore rightly calls the victory of Yaweh worship by the Israelites over Baal worship by the Amorites the first great victory of the common people, for it meant the establishment of the religious sanctions to democracy, brotherhood and freedom.

So the struggle has gone on through the course of history, a democratic people projecting into their idea of the deity those social and spiritual qualities which were most highly developed in themselves. Each nobler and more just conception of God, therefore, becomes evidence of a new level of political life, and is in turn a *magna carta* of liberties yet to be won.

In the light of this undoubted law, the problem of theology in the twentieth century becomes twofold. First, the problem of imagining attributes of deity which are at least as democratic as the attributes of the most highly socialized man; and second, creating an idea of God which shall bring man up to a newer and finer level of social experience.

The old ideas of a God who created a spiritual aristocracy, who maintained partiality, whose sympathies were not as wide as the whole of humanity, are patently inadequate to meet the new needs. There is no mistaking the democratic instinct in the new man. He passions after freedom and brotherhood. He lays bare his heart and mind to the great human currents and exults in the tides of feeling which pour upon him, enriching and enlarging him. There is no mistaking the widening of sympathies, the greater sense of inclusiveness, the new solidarity of humanity. Such a humanity will no longer brook the imperious and fastidious God who has scorned the fellowship of most of his creatures in the past. A democratic people demand a democratic God, a robust deity who likes his universe, who hungers for fellowship, who is in and of and for the whole of life, whose sympathies are as broad as the "rounded catalog, divine, complete,"

> The devilish and the dark, the dying and diseased,
> The countless (nineteen-twentieths) low and evil, crude
>   and savage,
> The crazed, prisoners in jail, the horrible, rank, malignant,

(What is the part the wicked and the loathsome bear
    within earth's orbic scheme?)
Newts, crawling things in slime and mud, poisons,
The barren soil, the evil men, the slag and hideous rot.

The Universalist idea of God is that of a universal, impartial, immanent spirit whose nature is love. It is the largest thought the world has ever known; it is the most revolutionary doctrine ever proclaimed; it is the most expansive hope ever dreamed. This is the God of the modern man, and the God who is in modern man. This is no tribal deity of ancient divisive civilization, this is no God of the nation or of a chosen people, but the democratic creator of the solid, indivisible world of rich and poor, black and white, good and bad, strong and weak, Jew and Gentile, bond and free; such a faith is as much a victory for the common people as was the passage of the Fourteenth Amendment to the Constitution. It carries with it a guarantee of spiritual liberties which are precedent to outward forms of governmental action.

From the summit of our muezzin towers we have seen this "glory that transfigures you and me," we have caught the larger vision, the mightier urge. The world hungers for this larger God. Nothing less will satisfy its longing. Nor height, nor depth, nor peril, nor nakedness, nor sword, nor any other creation shall separate us from the love of this, our God and Father. The swelling democracy of our age, like a roaring torrent, sweeps away the petty household idols, the national deities, the Calvinistic God, the small, defeated, limitarian Creator of the ages past, and bears our high imaginings on to the utmost periphery of all time, all space, and there trumpets the mighty, the triumphant God.

And not only is the Universalist conception of the Universal Fatherhood of God a response to the hunger for a larger, more democratic Creator, but it in turn begets a higher level of social life. A universal faith demands a universal application. This vast idea cannot be confined in one human mind, or in one favored class, but escapes beyond the narrow limitations of individualism into every conceivable relation of life. It cannot be calmly accepted by one and denied to the many. The Universal God means universal life, universal opportunity. It means the destruction of the olden tyrannies and the emancipation of the common man, Christ-like, free. It means the wreck of exploitation, the ruin of aristocracy; it means the exaltation of the meanest and weakest of God's creatures to the height of fulfillment. It means democracy.

Some timid folk shudder at the thought of their own innate greatness. From such the shackles of slavish thought would be struck, and into their blood would tingle and flow fresh streams of the glorious liberty of the sons of God. Others shiver at the vision lest it mean equality, and their accustomed prestige be broken. Many of them may well shiver if their prestige and power are won at the cost of exploitation or greed. Their hour has struck. They are doomed by democracy. But those whose power is that of justice, those who have gained their influence through superior capabilities of love and service, need fear nothing. The new age will crown them, and hail them as the true princes, potentates and kings.

The Universal Fatherhood of God, which clearly implies democracy, does not imply equality, for equality does not appear in nature. The infinite variety of the forms of life is occasion for perennial astonishment. Human beings exhibit the widest conceivable variety of physical and temperamental differences, which are not merely accidents of clime, but which are innate, and, so far as we can perceive, a part of the design of creation. Just as there are no two grains of sand alike and no two leaves alike, so there are no two men alike, and where there is no similarity there can be no equality. Democracy does not mean equality. It means the very opposite; its primary aim, in the definition of Dr. [Charles] Fleischer, is "the organization of society with respect to the individual." Democracy is an attempt to preserve whatever differences are innate and divine in human personality and to secure to all absolute freedom to become their own best selves.

The Universal Fatherhood of God recognizes the difference between the black and the white, but it declares that the fact of the difference is no ground for exploitation, but is rather an occasion for mutual respect and mutual self-fulfillment. The whole pith of the matter is this: that the differences which are innate in humanity are just, and must be clearly differentiated from the artificial distinctions which are superimposed upon humanity unjustly by men.

The idea of the Universal Fatherhood of God pulls society up to the higher levels of mutual respect, justice, brotherhood. It cannot be used as religious sanction for greed, injustice, slavery, caste, privilege. It is the common man's *magna carta* for political, social and economic opportunity to develop all the divine power with which God has endowed his regal soul.

Early in 1933, having been chosen dean of Crane Theological School, Skinner met with the Boston Universalist ministers and speculated on some challenges the school might face. In his address, "The Universalist Church Twenty-Five Years Hence," he perceived divergent conservative and "socially creative" wings of the church, technological changes, the labor movement, the value of the scientific method, psychological counseling, experiments in preaching and worship. He recommended that certain congregations be laboratories for new methods.

Even in this summary form, we can perceive Skinner's wide-ranging imagination and sensitivity to changes in the nation that could affect the practice of ministry. The reporter's final sentence displays a great respect for Skinner's vision. The article was published in The Christian Leader, *January 21, 1933, in the last days of the Hoover administration.—JDH*

Dean Skinner to Universalists

Some twenty-five ministers of the Universalist Church came through the storm January 9 to the regular session of the Boston Ministers' Meeting to hear Dean-elect Clarence R. Skinner of the Theological School of Tufts College on "The Universalist Church Twenty-five Years Hence."

The meeting was held in the Church of the Redemption. Dr. Huntley, president, . . . introduced Dean Skinner as a man of courage. Dean Skinner said in part:

"Any one who attempts prophecy must be very courageous or very humble.

"Technological change does not involve simply machinery. It involves thinking, living, working. It will change our attitude to life. It is natural for us who are brought up in certain ways of thinking to believe such ways can not change. Whoever looks back far enough in history will see how steadily changes come.

"There will be two significant movements in the religious world in the next few years, and both of these movements will divide the Universalist Church. In fact there is no Universalist Church. There are Universalist churches. I do not believe it possible to unify the Universalist Church any more than it is possible to unify the Presbyterian Church.

"One wing of the Universalist Church will become more conservative, in economic outlook, in social philosophy, in worship. And the more radical the social changes the more conservative these churches will become. I could pick out individual churches today and tell you which way they will go. Other Universalist churches, because of both laymen and ministers, because of lack of wealth, will drift toward the left sociologically and theologically. The great social problems are dividing people. The old unities are breaking up. Every one who has been an official in the Universalist fellowship must know these things to be true.

"The great question is: Do the Universalist churches want to be socially creative, and help mold the standards of the future? Or do they want to hold on to the best of the past? Do we want to be molders of a future society quite different from society as we know it, and so be creators, or do we not? If we do, we must put ourselves in line with forces that are strange or hostile to the church as we have known it in the past.

"The economic class movement, the labor movement, is working for a new order. If the Universalist Church wants to have a part in the future, it must get in line with these class movements.

"I do not look for a Bolshevik communism to control in the United States, but I do look for a working class movement to transform society. The church that wants to be creative must get into it.

"Science is making great strides. The nonscientific way of thinking is rapidly disappearing. A whole generation is coming into our colleges that has not spent one hour bothering with things outside the realm of fact. You must have observed this realistic trend. We have a generation that wants to know *what* more than it does *why* or *when*. It wants to base all programs on scientific analyses.

"I am saying hard things. I am saying partial things. I know they are partial.

"Young people are approaching problems not from the standpoint of what did Jesus say, or what does the Bible say, but from the standpoint of what does science say.

"I think ministers can be too devoted to science. I believe religion has a basis other than that in science. But the scientific method must control our thinking if we are to serve in the new day. There again will not the Universalist Church split? Can the two wings hold together?

"There is a new psychological approach and a new individualism. To see the best psychiatrists even now you have to make appointments two or three years in advance. People are not going to the church to find the solution of their problem unless the church employs the method of the psychologist. We are beholding a new generation, more honest, more free from false sexual ideals and ideas, more fearless.

"Here again the church will split. Some will make the new approach to the individual. Some will not. We must make it if we are to remain liberal.

"We must look forward to a time when the church will change so radically that preaching may disappear. The Christian Science Church has made the greatest progress in the past fifty years. It has no preaching.

"There has got to be a profound change in the technique of church life, and specialized men will have to be developed for special departments.

"I do not believe that preaching will disappear. I hope it will not. [Harry Emerson] Fosdick preaches to ten million every Sunday. But consider how efficient Christian Science has been and how inefficient some of the rest of us have been, and face frankly this possibility of a new organization without preaching.

"I want to ask you whether there is anything divine or sacrosanct about the kind of service we have. Do you realize that we have not made any real change in Universalist worship for one hundred years? Think about whether these forms that we use have any necessary validity. Can you not conceive of a service entirely different and vastly more efficient? I am coming to believe we can have a much more spiritual service without our old forms.

"If the General Electric were presented with the problems confronting us, they would proceed in a scientific way. They would set aside men to try things out. Why can't we do that in the Universalist denomination? Why should all new things come down from above—from teachers or officials of the denomination? Why not have special churches acting as laboratories?

"I'd like to see one Universalist church have the method of trying many men as preachers, putting in some other man as a parish worker. It might be tried in church like this. I'd like to see such a church made a liberal platform of preaching, the greatest men we can find employed, and see what happens. Would it be possible to experiment thoroughly with a Sunday evening forum? [Clinton] Scott in Peoria would be the type of man to try it. Try it for five years backed by the denomination, and publish the findings. I'd like to try an experiment in some beautiful church like this—have no preaching, but ritual, poetry, lights, colors, dramatics. That is, try the esthetic service.

"It would be far sounder to put denominational money into some of these experiments than into keeping alive churches bound to go down soon anyway.

"Then I'd try the experiment of making the church an educational center. Take the method of the Christian Scientist. Get a book. Try to put in a definite philosophy by a study method. Then after studying all the week come together as a class on Sunday with the minister as a leader. Publish all the results for the benefit of the rest of us. Possibly [the Universalist church in] Melrose could put in a psychological clinic. Then I'd like to have our ablest men find out why such and such a man is so greatly beloved in his church.

"Let all these things be reported on in five years, or ten years. Ministers then will have data to go on. They will know scientifically why this succeeds here and fails there. This will look forward to unification of weaker churches with stronger churches. The stress of time is crowding more churches to the wall. Others will fail. Perhaps if we planned we could put the churches together and employ two or three specialists.

"I see dangers in the Free Church of America [a short-lived liberal religious umbrella organization]. I see dangers in uniting churches and dangers in not uniting. The danger in not uniting is churches going on so feebly that they serve no useful purpose. The danger in union is that we may make a greater body of conservative opinion. That tendency may be seen in the Unitarian body today."

Dean Skinner generously gave time for a question period and the meeting closed with the general feeling that in years to come men would recall the day.

Throughout his career, Skinner created symposia and dialogic situations. Early in 1939, the Crane faculty took turns lecturing on the themes of religion, Christianity, the church, the Bible, worship, faith, and immortality. These were published as The Tufts Papers on Religion. *Dean Skinner led with "What Religion Means to Me," on this occasion emphasizing not social implications but the psychology of religious experience: "As partial experience gives way to universal experience we find man growing in wisdom, dignity, and morality."—JDH*

What Religion Means to Me

Religion. It is a word which inspires and confuses. It rouses passionate loyalties and equally passionate hatreds. There are those who see in it mankind sunk to its lowest depths of degradation. To some it is sublimely rational; to others it is stupid superstition. Theologians tell us that the world without religion would lose the highest values which keep man aspiring toward the best, and materialists tell us that without religion the world would be freed of the chains which bind it in slavery.

What is the meaning of this elusive, contradictory force which has wrought such strange results in the lives of individuals and in society? Are we able to experience it in this day and generation? Upon the answer hang momentous decisions, both for the present and for the future, for the individual and for society.

These questions are significant and important. They will not be lightly brushed aside, nor will indifference force them into complete silence. They are persistent problems for millions of people who attend services of religion, read about religion, discuss it, try to live it, and sincerely endeavor to wring from it the secrets which the great of old have found in it.

Ask ten people what religion is, and perhaps eight will reply uncertainly or will evade the questions altogether. Their answers, if attempted, are often intellectually muddled and emotionally embarrassed.

On the other hand, perhaps the answer will be so readily and glibly given that it betrays a mere cliché, an unthinking repetition of lifeless formulas. Ask these people what religion does for them and again they may be embarrassed, noncommittal, evasive. Can they assert with conviction that because they have taken part in the services of religion they are in any concrete way different persons than they would have been if they had not participated in such services? Do their religious beliefs really matter?

What does religion mean to me? I answer that question in genuine humility.

Religion is something which exhibits infinite variety. It manifests itself under continually changing forms. I am content not to give it exclusive, narrow definition. As a wild bird prisoned in a cage will often refuse to sing, so the highest values, when dissected and confined within the bars of precise definition, will cease to function. Certain it is that the logician with his net cannot always capture art, love, personality, or religion. Just when he thinks he has them in his toils, they escape into the freer air of real life.

I am torn between forces: one making for intellectual clarity, the other making for depth and reality of experience. On the one hand, I do not want to lend myself to those who make for obscurantism by retreating into a welter of undirected emotionalism. On the other hand, I am inclined to believe that "in divinity and love what's best worth saying cannot be said." My answer to this dilemma is to be as clear and intelligent as possible about religion as it enters into my own life, but to be generous in allowance for differences in others.

Religion means to me the reverent attitude to whatever seems to the worshiper the greatest and best. It is not a mere subjective enthusiasm or glow of satisfaction, nor it is necessarily devotion to one objective reality whom we must call "God." It is both subjective and objective.

I feel something which is a profound and beautiful emotion. Frankly, gladly, I let that emotion become a part of my experience. I am not ashamed of it, or afraid of it, nor am I too greatly distressed if I cannot always define it or see all of its logical implications. It is closely allied to awe, love, worship, idealization, yearning.

My emotion is directed toward something. It has an object which is outside myself. That object is not always the same, nor do I always react in the same way to the same object. Under various conditions, at different times and in different moods, my greatest and best changes. But always it is something outside myself which calls to me, as I call upon it. Man is never without a something beyond himself toward which he aspires. In religion it is not the name of the object which counts most, but the active spiritual relationship between the soul of a man and that something. In religion it is not so much the achievement that is important as it is that man forever aspires, reaches and towers beyond himself.

I find great personal satisfaction in [Alfred North] Whitehead's inspiring passage: "Religion is the vision of something which stands beyond, behind, and within the passing flux of immediate things; something which is real and yet waiting to be realized; something which is a remote possibility and yet the greatest of present facts; something that gives meaning to all that passes, and yet eludes apprehension; something whose possession is the final good, and yet is beyond all reach." ("Science and the Modern World.")

It has been said repeatedly and insistently that religion is a way of life. It is that, but that statement does not differentiate religion from numerous other "ways of life." Agriculture, laboratory analysis and crime are ways of life, but they are not necessarily identified with religion. In the religious consciousness we find something more than morals, art, or social legislation. These are not excluded. They may be parts, but they are not the whole. Religion seizes upon almost any experience and lifts it into an ideal end which, as [John] Dewey says, is pursued "against obstacles and in spite of threats of personal loss, because of conviction of its general and enduring value." ("A Common Faith.")

Some individuals may consider a hero or a loved one as the highest which imagination is capable of conceiving. If so, all the essential elements of religion are present in the experience: there are the emotional tensions of wistful yearning, the search for an object greater and better than himself.

We find this in Rama-krishna, a Hindu saint, as he knelt in single devotion and complete adoration of Mother Kali. Is not the reverent attitude of the Buddhist toward Gautama the essence of religion? For him the "Enlightened One" symbolizes the highest and holiest that he knows. Surely the undying loyalties of the devout Christian as he kneels before the figure of Christ are the very stuff of religious experience. Man-god or god-man has become a symbol of such high virtue and enduring worth that his personality expresses the greatest and best that some men can conceive.

Who does not feel the religious experience when he follows the career of Gandhi, when he reads of the beautiful life of St. Francis, or when he listens to the passionate appeal of Romain Rolland for a world of peace and internationalism?

Others may make religion of a group, such as a tribe or nation. It is hardly possible to read the lives of the great nationalists without realizing how close is their sense of devotion and sacrifice to that of religion. Limited their vision may be, but if the nation is the highest and best they know, their reverence before its symbols, their yearning for its glorification, contain all the elements of a religious experience. Marred by war as the history of nationalism has been, nevertheless it represents to millions the focus of their idealization and the expression of what is deepest in their lives.

To Joan of Arc, perhaps to a Hitler, nationalism may represent the will of God—the summation of ideal values for which they will gladly endure persecution and surrender their lives.

Some there are today who go beyond the confines of narrow race or warring state to bow before something far more majestic and awe-inspiring—humanity. The whole human race, past, present, and to come; not one divine person only, but all men and women, symbols of the highest. Scientists starving for truth, poets living in rags for love of supernal beauty, mothers clinging to their helpless brood, heroes dying in fire and flood, these are the greatest and best some men know. [Auguste] Comte, in the nineteenth century, worked out a religious service for the worship of humanity. Today many of the humanists declare that for them mankind stands at the end of their vista. It is the periphery of imagination: its struggles, defeats, hopes, and victories represent the holiest that we know. To get into the great stream of history, to sweat and sacrifice for truth, justice, and love—this is man at perihelion, this surely is religion enough.

Whosoever cannot be lifted unto heights by this magnificent concept must be dull and unimaginative. Man's continual struggle for justice, his blazing wrath at wrong, his vision of a world of brotherhood—these are the very stuff of religion. They reveal man bowing before an ideal and utterly dedicating himself to it. The ideal enters into a man's inner nature, lifts it, broadens it, and fills it with undying flame.

There are some, however, who feel that they must go beyond even this inspiring vision. Their imaginations urge their search "to vaster issues," and the soul is restless until it has moved out to the uttermost boundaries of the universe. It will be satisfied with nothing less than the whole of reality. It feels kinship with atoms, persons, social movements, and galaxies of stars wheeling in silent majesty across infinitudes of space. This is the highest reach of the human intellect, this is the profoundest reality of the human soul, this is the greatest and best man can know. It is symbolized by the great word "God," but the word is not the reality. It is the experience that counts. Man is caught up into a sublimity that lifts him, liberates his deepest self, stretches his imagination till it touches east and west, includes high and low, inspires and enriches him. This is the ultimate religion. In the great words of the poet [Samuel Taylor] Coleridge:

'Tis the sublime of man, his noon-tide majesty,
To know himself parts and proportions of one wondrous whole.

To me the highest type of religious experience is that which gives man a sense of unity and universality. Most of our life is spent in narrow segments. Our horizon is hemmed about by kitchen walls, office desks, narrow prejudices of race, class or creed. In religion, these partialisms, broken fragments of life, are lifted into a vast and profound oneness. Our littleness becomes stretched to cosmic greatness. Elemental forces roll through our beings, sensitize our perceiving, and quicken our lives. By a flash of insight we see in common things

The types and symbols of Eternity,
Of first, and last, and midst, and without end.

The spectroscope reveals the fact that man's body is made of the same elements as the farthest star. Chemistry proclaims man's kinship with the universe. Religious insight revealed centuries ago what physics and chemistry tardily proclaim. Man, from smallest cell to his total personality, is akin to the cosmos. We feel

Our destiny, our nature, and our home
Is with infinitude, and only these.

But one may say, men have stuck daggers into each other's hearts because they differed from each other as to the definition and description of this awful reality, or sublime being. As Lewis Browne graphically puts it in his description of Holy Jerusalem: "They have killed in this ancient town, killed until every alley was flooded with blood. Not a wall in all this maze of walls but has rung with the groans of the dying. Skulls beyond counting have been cracked on these flags; throats unnumbered have been slit in these dark doorways. They have murdered and pillaged and raped in this old holy town till now it is all but one Golgotha, one bloody hill of skulls. . . . And if you would know why, you need only look into the eyes of those hurrying phantoms. Readily they will tell you, explicitly. Men have slaughtered and ravished in Jerusalem, because they had—religion. Men have gouged eyes and ripped bellies because they—believed." ("This Believing World," by Lewis Browne, page 22, Macmillan, 1930.)

This, however, does not invalidate the fact that religious experience has been and may be one of the profoundest and noblest experiences of the human race. A scalpel may be used to save a man's life or to destroy it. Chemistry may produce bread or bombs; this is no special problem of religion; it is a problem of human nature.

Religious emotions and enthusiasms may be made to serve either intolerant fear or the lovely life of peace and healing good will. The objective results of religion will depend upon the character and extent of our scientific knowledge, and the development of our philosophy, ethics, and sociology.

Central and imperative in the religious problem is the question, how is religion integrated into the rest of life? What part do reason, truth, and goodness play in this great experience which has been so universal? This question is what confounds so many, turning some to bitterness, and others to obscurantism.

Every aspect of life is inextricably bound to every other aspect. The individual and the social, the true and the beautiful, reason and emotion, are all facets of one reality. The interaction is inevitable. The best life is one that is integrated, a life which makes a consistent whole out of religion, science, art, ethics, the individual and the social. In this kind of unified life, science does not defy art or religion. Economics does not defy beauty or philosophy. Each makes its distinctive contributions to an harmonious whole. What is good for one must be good for all. What is true for one must be true for all.

Such a view saves religion from murderous fanaticism or ignorant superstition. It redeems from ugliness or individualism.

The problem of directing and integrating religion is no greater than the problem of directing and integrating science or economics. Science in the hands of selfish and brutal men can be prostituted to the ends of rapine and crime. Industrialism can be made to plunder and starve. Even beauty may be made to serve the ends of sensuous passion. The parts must serve the whole, and the whole must keep the parts functioning in relation to each other.

To me, religion (which in Latin means "I bind") is a force which lifts every individual and every aspect of culture into a unified whole. When one glimpses the meaning of the universal, the inner conflicts are resolved. Races, creeds, science and beauty are integrated into harmony. To me the possession of a universal point of view is the highest achievement of man. In it I find the solution of our most perplexing problems. As partial experience gives way to universal experience we find man growing in wisdom, dignity, and morality.

In "Will Truth Make Us Free?" Skinner discusses the problem of specialization and integration of knowledge, examining the relation of university education to religion and a parallel discussion of the relation of truth to virtue. In this address he uses a dialogical form, playing one side against the other and seeking an inclusive synthesis. It was published in The Christian Leader, *July 3, 1943, and distributed to churches in pamphlet form.—JDH*

Will Truth Make Us Free?

"Ye shall know the truth, and the truth shall make you free."

—JOHN 8:32

There is always a danger that we shall become complacent about optimistic promises. We intensely desire a better world, therefore we are apt to believe the prophet who proclaims one. We want goodness to triumph over evil, and we hope that truth will conquer error, so when a great teacher assures us that these things shall be, we hear him gladly and our minds are put at rest. We confound promise with reality. Consequently, one of our continuing needs is to challenge all statements which tend to make us comfortably satisfied.

I have therefore taken upon myself the task of challenging Jesus' statement about the truth.

A minister usually preaches a sermon to prove his text. Today, however, I shall take the liberty of reversing the normal process and try to disprove my text.

In order to do this, may I first ask your indulgence and patience while we review briefly a certain phase of history which bears directly upon my task. This excursion may at first seem far removed from the problem which I have proposed, but I am sure that if you follow the argument with me, you will see that it does bear vitally upon the question.

Since the earliest days of which we have any record, man has been undergoing a process of specialization. At first the rate of differentiation was very slow. Each man and woman worked at a great variety of tasks. They were in turn hunters, fishers, agriculturists, doctors, manufacturers of clothing, carpenters, cooks, naturalists and philosophers. Consequently, all people in a community entered to a large degree into the shared experience of the common life. There was a maximum degree of integration of ideas and activities. Science, religion, and art were closely intertwined and fused into a living unity. Slowly, however, it was discovered that by doing fewer things more frequently, the worker gained in technical efficiency. The hunter became expert with bow and arrow, the medicine man with herbs and incantations. Some specialized in raising food, others in cooking it. A few men were even set aside for the business of thinking. Theirs was the task of pondering the problems of life and seeking solutions to the baffling contradictions and confusions which always arise in a dynamic world. They have become the truth seekers, progenitors of our philosophers and universities.

Every time the field of interest and activity was narrowed it became easier for an individual to master the intricate questions of knowledge and of use within that field. Obviously, by giving one's whole time and attention to building canoes, the builder learned more about materials and skills than if he had spent his life performing a large number of unspecialized tasks connected with every phase of economic, domestic and philosophic activity. Every one of these processes of specializing, however, was accompanied by a weakening of a sense of sharing the community life. Forces of unification gave way to forces of diversification.

Some of our theorists declare that the necessary interdependence which followed compensated for this lack of integration—which is partly true, but only in part. The psychological results of working and living in separate areas inevitably create misunderstandings and open unbridged chasms of estrangement.

As we all know, this process of specialization has been going on at an accelerated rate of speed, until today we have arrived at the age of the specialist. Instead of making automobiles, a worker pounds one bolt, and instead of building houses, workmen lay bricks or install plumbing. The most striking illustration of this tendency that I have ever heard is contained in a story about a famous eye specialist who was lecturing before a group of physicians. He stated that he had spent his whole life in this one narrow field, but confessed that he had not been able to master all the diseases of the eye. During his lecture he expressed the wish that at the beginning of his experience he had confined his labors to the covering of the eye. Then, perhaps, he would be master of the problems which now baffled him.

This process of differentiation has been going on not only *within* but also *between* certain areas of human activity. We now set aside a group of persons, for instance, who become expert in law and we give to them the task of maintaining and defining justice. The result is that today the average person can neither read nor understand a legal statute. Another group of persons called artists specialize in producing beauty and so esoteric do they become that poor John Q. Citizen has to be instructed in the reasons why a certain musical composition is beautiful. He must also submit to a guide who conducts him through the art museum and points out which is the top and which is the bottom of the picture and why.

The interdependence of interests which results from specialization does not guarantee a psychological sharing. The process of integration is imperfect. Chasms of misunderstanding and estrangement are bound to open.

My purpose today, however, is to speak of two examples of this specialization; namely, education and religion; and to indicate some of the dangers of their separation.

The university, as the organized expression of education, has gradually been set aside from other institutions to devote itself to the highly differentiated task of seeking, discovering, and imparting truth. The motto of the university is, "Ye shall know the truth and it shall make you free." Increasingly the energies of modern faculties go into research, and the object of research is to discover facts.

There are two reasons why we want to know the truth. One is because there is a hunger of the mind to know. Curiosity drives us to analyze and discover. The object of this search is not always utilitarian. We love the truth because it is true. The rational faculties point to truth as the magnetic needle points to the north. We serve truth because it lays hold upon us and commands us. Thus, in devoting our lives to truth and in building institutions dedicated to the pursuit of knowledge, we satisfy one of the deepest cravings of the spirit, and we exemplify one of the noblest qualities of man.

The other reason which especially concerns us today is because we want to be free. By understanding the laws of the universe we can be emancipated from superstition and error. We can increase power and multiply satisfactions in proportion to our control over the forces of human nature, society and the universe. By understanding disease, we gain health. By understanding electricity, we bid unseen slaves sweat for us. By finding out the secrets of the atoms, we create new plastics which may serve man in innumerable ways. Therefore, we want to know the truth so that the truth will make us free.

But now I come to the main point of my sermon, and I thrust this sharp question into your minds—does truth make us free?

Look about you and see for yourself. I fear no contradiction when I say that the twentieth century has seen more discovery of truth than any equal period of time in human history. Yet the inescapable fact is that we are not free. We live under more terror than ever before. We are enslaved on an unprecedented scale. Starvation and disease are engulfing literally tens of millions. Our planes of living are going down. We must toil harder and longer, we must suffer more restrictions. We are not free. Yet we know more truth. What is the matter?

I should like to answer this question under two heads: First, when we specialize truth to an excessive degree we cut it off from its life context and make it impotent. Knowledge alone is not always power. Sometimes it is mere pride or ornamentation. It may lead to dilettantism. It certainly may be wholly ineffective in making a better world. If I say to a drug addict: "Sir, your physiological system is shattered because you have taken more drugs than you can stand," will he immediately become free? Far from it! The mere fact of knowing does not necessarily bring deliverance. Even if we have curative medicines at hand the victim does not necessarily avail himself of their powers.

We know that slums breed disease, cause crime, frustrate man's desire for a good life, and we know that they are not economically sound. Does that make us free? Far from it! There are hundreds of thousands of people living in squalor and utter wretchedness in our crowded cities despite what we know about slums.

We know that war is wasteful, antiquated, self-defeating and destructive of human values. Yet literally millions of men, women and children are being torn into bloody shreds of flesh, and millions more will be offered to this Moloch. Does our knowledge of the wickedness of war make us free from its ravages? Far from it!

It is obvious, then, that merely knowing is not enough. Perhaps our universities have forgotten this fact, and by specializing to so great a degree have removed truth from its life context and have thus made it comparatively impotent. Many an animal when brought in from the woods and confined in a cage has sickened and died. Often plants taken from the fields and put into hothouses wither and pass away. So with truth. When taken out of its context in real life it, too, loses vitality.

It misses the environment in which it naturally flourishes. It lacks a sense of robust reality. It becomes anemic and pale.

Life is one. It cannot be successfully departmentalized. The good, the true and the beautiful are inseparably connected. Truth must be related to the good and the beautiful. Goodness must be made beautiful and true. Beauty must be guided by truth and goodness. Any one of these cut off from the others may defeat itself. Truth may become evil; goodness, erratic; and beauty, sensuous.

All knowledge and all virtue must be integrated into a living unity. If education be so specialized that it speaks a language foreign to life, if it becomes so rarefied that it does not meet the pressing needs of men, then it becomes unreal— a ghostly wraith which haunts the chambers of learning.

Truth is not a pure abstraction, existing in a vacuum. It is of the earth earthy. It resides in relationships and in concrete realities. In order to produce results it must be tied into situations where tensions arise and it must become a part of a complex unity.

If we are to become free, truth must get into the world of politics, economics, agriculture, business and family life. Perhaps Matthew Arnold gave us one of our greatest ideals when he spoke of the need of "seeing life steadily and seeing it whole." This is what I am pleading for in relation to knowledge. It must become an integrated part of the stream of life. It must not be so specialized that no one can visualize its effects and uses. The discovery and development of truth should go hand in hand with a realization of what its relationships may be.

Perhaps one of the best illustrations of this point is the discovery of dynamite. [Alfred] Nobel learned a truth and he gave it to the world. He did not ask how it might fit into the total scheme of society. Too late he saw the horror and destruction which truth would bring to humanity. The Nobel Peace Prizes were ineffective. The harm had been done. The discoverer of dynamite had not seen life steadily and seen it whole.

So with the submarine, the airplane, poison gas and other examples too numerous to list. These may make us free, but they can also destroy us. It depends upon our integration of truth into goodness and beauty. Truth may slay us, or it may save us. There is no guarantee in truth itself that it will do either.

We have now reached a momentous period in man's development, when we must decide whether the truth is to be free to make us slaves or whether we are to control truth to make us free.

Again, in order to win freedom, truth must be linked to action. Knowledge which ends in itself defies one of the first laws of psychology; namely, that when we feel an emotion or experience a rising tension, we ought to provide a wholesome and useful outlet for it. Professor [William] James long ago told us that when we are inspired by a beautiful symphony we ought to go home and speak a kind word to our mother-in-law.

There is a danger that truth today may become departmentalized and esoteric. It doesn't speak to its mother-in-law. In fact, it does not even realize that family relatives exist. It prides itself upon being so specialized that the average man cannot understand its language. The danger is that it will develop its cult and devotees who form an unworldly priesthood withdrawn into the sacred precincts of learning and remain there for life.

Some of you may fear that I am preaching a gospel of utilitarianism and making a plea for a system where every truth must be compelled to declare a dividend in terms of material results. Far from it! I am, however, making a strong plea for a healthy, robust kind of knowledge which bears fruit in freedom—a knowledge which goes out from the halls of learning into the world of reality.

Let me illustrate from an actual instance which has come under my observation. A certain university signed a contract with a business firm to build a concrete walk on its campus. This walk led from the engineering school to the main road.

Faculty members who were experts in the field of building materials used to spend part of their noon hour watching the process of mixing and laying the cement. They all agreed that the materials were below standard, that the path would disintegrate rapidly, and that the work would have to be done over again in a very short time. Yet the contractor went on with his shoddy work, and the truth remained locked up in the brains of the university professors.

This instance is but a symbol of our failure so to organize our knowledge that it shall lead to freedom. We know enough about tuberculosis to exterminate it, but still its ravages go on. We know enough about architecture to eliminate slums, but still they exist. We know enough about agriculture to feed the world, but millions continue to starve. We have sufficient knowledge of production techniques to give every man and woman and child in the world a good living, but vast numbers are in grinding poverty. We have the skills to bring about education and a cultural standard for all, but most people even in this rich country do not go to high school. We know enough about sociology to prevent a large degree of crime, but today we are making juvenile delinquents on an unprecedented scale.

Truth sometimes suffers from paralysis, and when that happens, it fails to make progress. It becomes introvert and static.

So I might go on endlessly pointing out the fact that when truth does not lead to action, it does not make us free.

A few minutes ago I said that not only education but also religion had suffered from specialization, and I shall now proceed to speak briefly of that fact and its significance, especially in relation to the truth.

Just as the university is prone to become esoteric, so is the church. Religious customs and practices were at first largely shared by members of the family and by all dwellers in the community. Religion was a common concern to everybody and it was integrated into art, economics, marriage, birth and death. It was a vital part of everyday life. Gradually, however, the same process of differentiation that we have seen in regard to truth begins to affect religion.

Into the hands of the priest were delivered certain mysteries and practices which tended to become highly specialized. In the early development of the race, men entrusted to their religious leaders the formulas and prayers which must be said with meticulous care in order to keep the universe going. If the priest mispronounced a word of the ritual, the sun would not rise. If he made a mistake in the sacrifice, God would visit the people with his wrath.

The priest thus gradually became cut off from the nourishing roots of reality. His language became unknown to his people. His profession became highly technical, and he began to surround both his person and his ideas with an estrangement which set him apart from his fellows. He developed ritualism which was far removed from truth. His goodness even became obscurant and often served to keep men in ignorance and thus in intellectual as well as spiritual slavery. Goodness which becomes specialized from truth is built on such a shaky basis that it cannot bear the weight of reality. It crumples up and collapses. It does not make men free.

An illustration is to be found in the often repeated doctrine that at midnight on a certain day and year the world will come to an end. Belief in this cataclysmic event has flourished like the green bay tree and will again flourish as men turn toward an apocalyptic type of religion. It exhorts men to repentance, to cleanse the thoughts of their hearts from all sin and vice, and to prepare for God's judgment. Undoubtedly it preaches goodness, but a goodness which is so completely divorced from a true and sound conception of life that it becomes a power for evil.

So with faith. A revivalist in the Southern mountain regions exhorted his hearers to have faith that if bitten by a rattlesnake God would cure them. He called for volunteers and told them that if they did not come forward they would be self-convicted of doubting God's power and love. Goaded by this challenge, some men offered themselves for the experiment. They were bitten by rattlesnakes, refused a doctor's care and promptly died.

Faith is a basic virtue. It is fundamental to all religions, to all science, and to all life. But when it is cut off from truth it may lead us into mortal error. Faith may slay us and destroy our civilization. It may lend itself to blind emotionalism and social reaction. It may prompt men to surrender their wills to a dramatic but evil leader. It may persuade people to believe what is absurd and thus set up a warfare between reason and religion.

Take any virtue you will—hope, love, beauty or sympathy—separate it from its context in life and it may become disintegrative and destructive. Love can be pathological, hope can be fatuous, sympathy can be maudlin. Faith, hope and love, to become beneficial, must be integrated into all the normal processes of life. They must be unitary. They must not be specialized into anemic abstractions. They must not be like wild flowers brought from the woods and transplanted into the parlor, or like an animal brought from the jungle and condemned to a lifetime of incarceration.

Separate virtue from truth and it becomes a vice. Separate truth from virtue and it becomes a jailer.

Have I now proven my text to be unsound? Are you convinced that the truth does not make us free?

Wait a minute. Jesus put this great saying in the future tense. He did not say that truth *had* made us free in the past. He said it *shall* make us free. That statement is in the future tense. It seems to me that he was in effect saying that truth, under the proper conditions, should and could emancipate us. I don't mean to quibble with words or to persuade you to dance on the point of a scholastic's needle. This is important. It points to a distinction with a tremendous difference. I believe that Jesus spoke a great truth. You see that, after all, one very undistinguished preacher has not been exercising his egotism by pitting his poor intelligence against the great authority and insight of Jesus. "Ye *shall* know the truth, and the truth *shall* make you free." There is hope for humanity—not a hope that is fatuous and unrealistic, but a hope that is born of robust realism. The truth can make us free, but we must discover the proper conditions.

The way lies clear ahead. Unfetter truth from narrowing specializations. Link it to life, real life in all its varied aspects. Bring it out from the university into the crowded, struggling world and let it serve. Above all, let it again unite with righteousness that truth may be good, and goodness true.

Our contemporary civilization has been myopic. In developing techniques and means it has forgotten the Kingdom of Ends. We must learn to ask one fundamental question of every activity or interest, namely, does it serve some ultimate end which gives it validity? Wealth is assumed by many to be a good, but it is not necessarily so. It may be an evil unless we can be assured that it is related to a sound and wholesome purpose. As [John] Ruskin was fond of saying, much so-called wealth is really illth because it makes for the sickness of society. So with education, which many people assume to be the highest good. We have seen in Europe how education can be prostituted and made to serve the ends of destruction. So with many other so-called goods like freedom and initiative. What are we free for? Are we free to create dust-bowls and to destroy our natural resources? Has not Hitler shown initiative? How about criminals and exploiters?

Without overloading this brief sermon with too many illustrations, is it not clear that almost any form of good may serve evil? That virtue takes on its quality of goodness by serving the good end? That any person or any activity may become evil when he or it serves the evil end?

Our culture has trusted too much in facts. It has let science go where it will, serving heathen gods. But we are suffering for our sins. We are enslaved in an age of enlightenment because our enlightenment is not total. We are one-eyed philosophers and have lost the ability to see more than one thing at a time.

Shall we devote ourselves to truth? By all means! Shall we continue loyally to support and build universities? Without stint and without limit! Let us seek truth and pursue it with a passion that knows no bounds. But let us remember the great text of Paul: "For the wrath of God is revealed from heaven against all ungodliness and unrighteousness of men, *who hold the truth in unrighteousness.*"

There is the warning. And surely God has not left us in any doubt as to his wrath. But let us make another text by inverting Paul's words: "The blessing of God is revealed from heaven to all godliness and righteousness of men *who hold truth in righteousness.*"

There is the hope and the promise. A striking phrase in the Old Testament illustrates this thought: "Truth shall spring out of the earth; and righteousness shall look down from heaven." Must we say that earth is earth and heaven is heaven, truth is truth and righteousness is righteousness, and never the twain shall meet? Or shall we say that truth springs up to heaven and righteousness bends down to earth, and the two shall be wedded and become as one?

We can be free, we will be free, but only when these two great virtues have been integrated into an indivisible whole. Righteousness must be founded on truth. It must square with reality. It must harmonize with what we know of the universe. But truth must be righteous. It must serve the good and not the evil. It must seek the Kingdom of Ends. It must serve the moral law.

The University and the Church. Truth and righteousness. May they unite to bless men and turn this bleeding old earth into a heaven. "Ye shall know the truth, and the truth shall make you free."

Skinner's last completed book, A Religion for Greatness, *shows his mature vision of universal religion. Written in the midst of World War II, he transforms the significance of the word "Universalism" to represent a religion for all people. In Chapter 2, "The Religion of the Unities and the Universals," he speaks of "radical religion" in the sense of going to the roots: "Radical religion creates in many [people] a sense of vital, meaningful relationship between the self and the universe."*

His program has three themes: insight, unity, and universal. "Religion provides insight into these unities and universals." He charged the Universalists "to so expand our spiritual powers that we vastly increase the range of our understanding and sympathy. There is no middle way. It is greatness—universalism—or perish."

Skinner's final book, like his first, had a major impact on the Universalist Church, this time moving out beyond its Christian heritage toward a world religion, or a religion for the world.—JDH

The Religion of the Unities and the Universals

Man takes his norm from earth; earth from heaven; heaven from Tao; the Tao from itself.

—FROM THE *TAO-TEH-KING* (CHINESE)

The universe and I came into being together; and I, and all things therein, are One.

—CHUANG-TZE (CHINESE)

The all-working, all-wishing, all-smelling, all-tasting one, that embraceth the universe, that is silent, untroubled—that is my spirit within my heart: that is

Brahman. Thereunto, when I go hence, shall I attain.
— *CHANDOGYA-UPANISHAD* (HINDU)

God hath made of one every nation of men to dwell on all the face of the earth, having determined their appointed seasons and the bounds of their habitation, that they should seek God, if happily they might feel after him and find him, though he is not far from each one of us, for in him we live and move, and have our being.
—PAUL (CHRISTIAN)

That which is the cause of perfect unity and amity in the world of existence is the oneness of Reality.
—BAHAI

What, then, is this radical religion which goes down below surface appearance, and finds its root in the profoundest reality? How do we realize it in our lives? What have been some of its manifestations in history, and do we find that it has really been a common experience?

To sum the answer in a word, radical religion creates in man a sense of vital, meaningful relationship between the self and the universe. In primitive man this feeling may center in worship of sun, moon, stars, or other natural phenomena. It may manifest itself by the belief in and practice of mana—an all-pervasive potency which endows men with unique gifts. No matter how crude and superstitious man's early religion may have been, it lifted him out of his isolation into union with powers and influences greater than himself. His religious experience gave him an orientation toward the unities and the universals. Groping through fogs of ignorance he laid hold on the central fact of human existence; namely, that there is a relationship of dependence between man and the powers which exist outside and beyond himself.

Radical religion does not insist upon naming or describing

these powers. Animism, polytheism, deism, theism, are phases of the essential experience, but none of these is necessary to it. The elemental fact is the outreach of man to something beyond himself.

What primitive man may have dimly apprehended has grown through the centuries into an increasingly clear conviction. The outreach has attained larger proportions, and our consciousness has broadened with the process of evolution. We have become less trustful of naive emotions, and hence more sophisticated. We want to name and define what we feel, but despite all obstacles radical religion persists.

A most interesting example of this elemental experience in modern life has recently been recorded by [William Ernest] Hocking:

A short time ago I was talking with a colleague, a psychiatrist. He said, "Something has been occurring to me recently which seems important, and yet it seems so simple that I can hardly believe it very significant. It is a way of taking the miscellany of events that make up the day's impressions of the world. One sees no trend in them. But suppose there were a trend that we cannot define but can nevertheless have an inkling of. There is certainly some direction in evolution, why not in history? If there were such a trend, then we men could be either with it or against it. To be with it would give a certain peace and settlement; to be against it would involve a subtle inner restlessness. To have confidence in it would be sort of a commitment, for better or for worse. I wonder if that is what you mean by religion."

"Yes," I said, "I think that is the substance of it. The great religious ones seem to have had a certainty that they were going along with the trend of the world. They have had a passion for *right living which they conceived of as a cosmic demand.*"[1]

"There is nothing contrary to science in that."

"No, but it makes a difference, doesn't it?"

"Strange that such a simple thing should make so very much difference."[2]

Such is the insight which comes to man, whether primitive or modern, whether naive or sophisticated.

Beneath all curious customs and beliefs, deeper than ecclesiastical creeds, more vital and basic than priestly rites, stands out one impressive fact—namely, man touches infinity; his home is in immensity; he lives, moves, and has his being in an eternity. This magnificent assertion is man's greatest affirmation. Nothing else surpasses it in sweep of imagination or depth of understanding. It is a truth proclaimed by all that we know of modern science, and it stands the test of experience as the enduring reality.

It is man's effective protest against all that lessens and divides. It is his emphatic denial of any attempt to separate him from his home and heritage. It expresses his uncompromising unwillingness to be reduced to insignificance and utter isolation. This radical interpretation would rescue religion from its fringes and accretions. It would scrape the barnacles off the elemental truth and reveal the basic reality in its purity and power. So many superficial impedimenta have been heaped upon religion by its devotees that it is frequently impossible to recognize the genuine from the spurious. But by rethinking religion and by performing a major surgical operation upon it, we can discover the vital organs. The radical interpretation refuses to be led aside by the extraneous. It insists upon returning to what is the essential core of religious experience; namely, the seeking after and finding man's relation to the unities and universals.

Three words will occur often in this essay; so often, in fact, that they may seem repetitious. To understand their meaning is vital to the understanding of the central theme of this essay. It will therefore be necessary to define these terms with as much precision as possible, and the reader is urged to fasten the definitions in his mind now, or to turn back to this page from time to time to refresh his memory.

The terms are of such a nature that they cannot be reduced to mathematical exactitude, but they are not so vague and discrete as to mean anything or nothing. They will be used with a certain connotation which is always in the mind of the author when he writes them.

Insight. The dictionary gives us the following: "A perception of the inner nature of a thing." In our view this ability may be purely intellectual, or it may be due to some causal factor which works in conjunction with intelligence. It may be close to intuition. Perhaps even some mystical quality may inhere in this ability to grasp the inner nature of some form of reality. Whatever the cause or character of the insight, we shall assume its validity when, like any other form of knowledge, we test it by empirical methods.

Unity. Again, the dictionary says, "The state of being indivisibly one; harmony, concord." This unity may be purely physical, as the unity of the human body; it may be intellectual, as the unity of a scheme or plan; it may be used as a metaphysical term, implying a fundamental unity underlying all aspects of reality. It may be used with all these meanings in this volume, but always it will mean the coherence of what may seem to be separate, into a oneness. Unity means an operative harmony, a functional relationship which belongs to all the parts of a whole.

Universal. Funk and Wagnalls says: "Relating to the entire universe; unlimited; general. Regarded as existing as a whole; entire. Including all of a logical class. A universal concept; that which may be predicated of many particular things or persons." We shall give all these connotations to the word. The universal will mean the all-inclusive as far as we can imagine it—the entire cosmos with all it contains. Again it will mean all of a class, as, a universal religion or a universal language. Finally, we shall mean by the term that which is the antithesis of the limited, or fragmentary. It is the opposite of the partial.

When we speak of universalism we shall mean a philosophy of life or system of values which stresses the largest possible *Weltanschauung,* or world outlook, in contrast to the narrow view which is herein denominated partialism.

To return now to the consideration of the main theme of this chapter; namely, the fact that religion provides insight into these unities and universals.

A glance at the quotations at the beginning of this chapter gives some intimation of this type of religion as expressed in many different cultures and by persons of differing periods of time.

Taoism, in its sacred scripture, the *Tao-teh-King,* gives a remarkable example of this insight: "Man takes his norm from earth; earth from heaven; heaven from Tao; the Tao from itself." Without going into a extended and unnecessary discussion of the meaning of the terms used by Lao-tse, the founder of the movement, we see at once the kind of philosophy, mysticism, which religion gives to a noble mind. Man is surrounded by earth and all its forces. To put it scientifically, we are geocentric. We are related to soil, climate, flora, fauna, and all the chemical and physical laws which operate on the earth. This planet however, is by no means an isolated fact. It swings in a vast cosmos, and so, as man takes his norm from earth, so the earth takes its norm from heaven. Needless to say, heaven did not mean to the Chinese twenty-five hundred years ago what it means today. The significant thing about the statement is not its astronomy, but its early insight into the fact of orderliness and interrelatedness. If heaven meant to Lao-tse some thing in the nature of a moral as well as physical order so much the better for our argument. It simply extends the sweep and scope of the author's insight into the unity of all phases of the universe, whether moral or physical. Heaven, however, is not an ultimate and final fact, but it, too, is dependent on something more elemental and self-sustaining. The Tao is the uncaused cause, the prime mover, the *Ding an sich* which all philosophers must assume as the ultimate reality. It gives measure, shape and meaning to all else, including the wide expanse of the cosmos, this planet, and even man, small as he may seem in the universal order of things.

It would be difficult indeed to find a more complete and satisfying statement of radical religion than this logical and penetrating summary by the sage Lao-tse.

This religio-philosophical type of thought is perhaps found at its best in Hinduism, and it evolves as early as the Upanishads. The Indian sages evolved the Brahman-atman doctrine, and considering the fact that the period in which it was conceived was prescientific, and taking into account the highly poetic form in which it is written, there never has been a more satisfying statement of man's cosmic nature.

The Brahman here means, as accurately as we can translate it, the soul of the universe—the fundamental principle which goes into the making of all things. It is the inner nature of the all-embracing, all-animating reality. Wisely, the Hindu refrains from describing this nature or Universal Self. He declares that names merely limit what is essentially limitless and put bounds to what is not to be bounded and defined by man's feeble vocabulary. Like the Tao in Chinese systems, it is not person-alized, yet it is not denied that it can be manifested in terms of personality. But whatever it is, it must be too great to be compassed about with things temporal and local.

On the other hand is the atman—the self of each indi-vidual—the inner reality which motivates human action, gives ground or foundation to our being, and sustains in us our life force. We in the West are accustomed to calling this the individuating principle the ego, or soul, which marks off one single person from all other persons. The Hindu sage, on the contrary, declares that this atman is not an isolated, unrelated entity standing apart from others. This separateness is an illusion and is at the root of most of our ills. The true atman is identic with the Brahman. The two are merged into one, and therein lies illumination and salvation for man. The ego is not an individual possession; it is simply part of the all.

The "I" which man so proudly proclaims is allied to the

plants and to the animals. What St. Francis was to express so beautifully centuries later in his Canticle to the Sun was a commonplace of Hindu thought a thousand years before our era. All life is sacred, because the soul of all is the soul of each.

By the same token, man is part of humanity. You are I and I am you. We are merged in the one environing and interpenetrating All. This fragmentary self, upon which we sometimes insist, is revengeful, cruel and inhuman only when it is ignorant of its unity with all other men. My life is not so much mine as a particle of the Infinite life encased for a passing moment in a frame which houses it in fragile solitariness. It is the drop of water lifted for a brief day by the lotus leaf from the pool. Soon the drop will fall back into the source whence it came—merged in water which is common not only to the one pool, but with all water everywhere. It becomes a crystal of snow on Mt. Everest, a drop in the Holy Ganges, or it reflects the Taj Mahal on a silvered moonlit night.

So it is with the ego's relation to infinity and eternity: whether incarnated in the form of a sacred cow or a perfect Buddha, whether toiling on a farm or sitting in quiet contemplation, under the beneficent stars, the soul feels itself to be one with the tides of life as they sweep through time and space.

> The everlasting universe of things
> Rolls through the mind.

Are these reflections of the oriental mere empty verbiage—sound and fury, signifying nothing? Are they to be cast out of consciousness as ancient and uncouth good, man's feeble attempts to lay hold on truth but long since outmoded?

Skip two thousand years and see where a devout soul has laid bare its inward promptings. All day he has been reading in science, immersed in the world of gritty fact. In the *Journal Intime* of Henri Frederic Amiel occurs the following passage which he wrote under the date of April 21, 1855:

I have traversed the universe from the deepest depths of the empyrean to the peristaltic movements of the atom in the elementary cell. I have felt myself expanding in the infinite, and enfranchised in spirit from the bounds of time and space, able to trace back the whole boundless creation to a point without dimensions, and seeing the vast multitude of suns, of milky ways, or stars, and nebulae, all existing in the point.

And on all sides stretched mysteries, marvels and prodigies without limit, without number, and without end. I felt the unfathomable thought of which the universe is the symbol live and turn within me; I touched, proved, tasted, embraced my nothingness and my immensity. I kissed the hem of the garments of God, and gave him thanks for being spirit and for being life. Such moments are glimpses of the divine. They make one conscious of one's immortality; they bring home to one that an eternity is not too much for the study of the thoughts and works of the eternal; they awaken in us an adoring ecstasy and the ardent humility of love.[3]

A cynical modern may lay aside such flowery and high-flown poetry as mere outpourings of an easily excited spirit. His imagination was fired by the slightest spark because he was quick to respond to any stimulus. Surely our cynic would say, this means nothing. Such a rush of words pouring pell-mell from a ready pen were simply the easing of a psychological tension. Words—empty of any profound insight into the nature of things deep and elemental.

Are they? Do we not find here, as in Taoism and in Hinduism, a flash of revealing which goes to the very core of truth and illumines the universe? Echoing the cry of Augustine for man's discovery of the ultimate, he continues:

There is no repose for the mind except in the Absolute; for feeling except in the Infinite; for the soul except in the Divine. Nothing finite is true, is interesting, is worthy to fix my attention. All that is particular is exclusive, and all that is exclusive repels me. There is nothing non-exclusive but the All; my end is communion with Being through the whole of being.[4]

How can any man read these truths wrung from the depths of a great man's life without feeling an immediate affirmation and confirmation? Not, of course, an exact agreement with every word and implied theological definition; but taking the intent, the large meaning of it all, how can we fail to feel the authenticity of such an insight? To read it reverently opens windows and unfolds vistas of high religion and solemn festival for the soul.

Dr. [Bernard] Meland expresses some clear convictions on this matter:

> Only those whose rootings reach deeply into the environing realities that sustain them, whose perspective is continually cleansed of self-centeredness, and whose mind and organism are kept plastic and expansive by experiences of awe, wonder and reverence, find the assurance and incentive to be inclusive. For inclusive attitudes, which issue in friendly and magnanimous conduct, have their psychological basis in an expansive organism. Back of every show of selfishness, greed, ruthlessness, or deceit is a contractive organism that clutches and holds things to itself. The source of its unsocial attitudes and conduct is the tension centering around the *I*. Ease the tension and you lessen the unsocial complex, for you then relax the egocentric focus. The importance of contemplative worship for conduct is therefore apparent. It turns man away from himself. It opens before him an expanse of reality so vast, so austere, and so significant, that it confounds his ego and punctures any inflation that might be forming or

existing in incipient form. It confronts him with a wealth of mystery that breaks through more sophistic allegiance to science, and crowds out dogmatisms. Contemplation thrusts us from our tiny thrones and renders us subjects of a greater kingdom. It dispels self-worship and turns us to a greater devotion, and in so doing it transforms our self-centeredness into a shared way of living.[5]

This passage seems to indicate something profoundly true and radical about religion, especially that type of religion which we have been describing. It is *expansive* in the very nature of its being. It is other-regarding. It adds a fourth dimension to our lives. The disciplines connected with religious living are therefore exactly what the world needs at this moment of crisis.

Compare such an enlarging and inclusive experience as worship or contemplation with the contracting influence of our acquisitive enterprises. Economic activities are closely related to the grasping nature of man. In the very nature of the case, getting a living is a problem of subtraction and of egocentricism. Pleasure, amusement, and hosts of daily activities, which make up routine for millions of lives, are self-centered. Their discipline tends to make man look within, or to focus the outside upon himself. This great religious experience of the unities and the universals, however, tends to direct man outward toward what is greater than the atomistic human.

Love, service, unselfish devotion to the common good, are all in line with the expansive experiences, but they are definitely limited in scope. Even at best their horizons are narrowly confined. But the religion of the universals and the unities has no felt limitations. It leads out to the infinite and thus tends to make the largest possible type of human personality. It would be hard to imagine a person with an habitual cosmic "mind-set" descending into the bitter and exclusive partialisms which divide men. The point of view and the psychological disciplines of the Universe-Man are inclusive and integrating.

This insight, experienced by men thousands of years ago, is authenticated by the findings of the laboratory. Let us take an example. If we turn a spectroscope on the farthest star, we get a series of light bands informing us of the chemical composition of that distant heavenly body. It is in the nature of a telegram informing the chemist as to the exact elements which are resident in sidereal matter. Very well. Turn this same instrument on man and we find the same light bands, indicating the identical chemical composition! What does that prove? Precisely this: Man and the universe are one. We reject the dichotomy that thrusts human kind into one separate category, completely isolate, and puts the stars into another fact world or frame of reference. A thread of unity runs through all.

Take the laws of physics for another example, and we find that here, again, we are confronted with a common world. When a man lifts his finger he obeys the same universal laws of force and matter as obtain on Jupiter or Betelgeuse. Let man raise a one pound rock three feet and he has raised the center of gravity of the earth; and when the gravity of the earth shifts, it affects the planets, and the orbits of the planets affect the stars, and the stars affect the solar systems, and the systems reach out into the universe.

It is small wonder that we grow bitter at man's sinful partialisms. We have every reason to be rebellious against the stupidity and cruelty which turn the Elysian fields into a charnel house. But one fact persists through all our disillusioning and through all our attempts to make man naught but a miserable worm—a damned spot, to be erased and forgotten. That fact is the cosmic affinity of this same man, who in the most brilliant moments of flashing genius rises above the pettiness and indignity of his lesser self to the stature of the All.

[Albert] Einstein, in his very brief essay entitled *Cosmic Religion*, says that there are three stages through which men pass in their religious development. First is the stage marked by fear of all the evils that beset mankind. A second and higher type evolves from the social feelings such as love and fellowship. Einstein believes that the anthropomorphic idea of God is common to these types, but there is a higher stage which he calls "cosmic religion." The individual feels "the nobility and marvelous order which are revealed in nature and in the world of thought. He *feels the individual destiny as an imprisonment and seeks to experience the totality of existence as a unity full of significance*."[6]

Here is a modern scientist, who certainly cannot be accused of sentimentality, recognizing just what we have been striving to express: man's existence and destiny as an individual (that is, as a separate unit) are a form of restriction and limitation. Separateness is an imprisonment. We find the meaning of human personality and the meaning of the whole universe in the unity of the parts with the whole. Just as a spark plug can be understood only when it is seen as part of an automobile, so man can be understood only when he is recognized as part of the universe.

Einstein tells us that "the religious geniuses of all times have been distinguished by this cosmic religious sense." Again, as we have been trying to say, the religious insight in its highest form perceives and conceives this quality of wholeness and inclusiveness, and believes it to be of the highest value.

Those who have experienced it in their personal lives have developed certain qualities which the world desperately needs. They have become "universe men" with an outlook so all-including that they can integrate into themselves all aspects of human, geographical, and even astronomical life. Examples of such personalities will be given in the next chapter. [His examples are Jesus, Peter, Paul, Albert Schweitzer, Walt Whitman, and Devendranath Tagore.]

It is the further thesis of this essay that such personalities logically develop a social outlook which again is the basic and imperative need of our day. Because such men and women have experienced something cosmic and emancipatory, they inevitably reach out beyond the partialisms and fragments of human relations to those forms and practices of social life which are the largest and most inclusive. Both theoretically and practically the larger faith is creative of a social universalism.

To borrow a magnificent phrase from Herbert Agar: "It is a time for greatness." The crisis of our age which is one of the most acute in the whole history of man might well be described as a sudden demand for greatness for which the world is not prepared. Our trade, our civilization, have become unified and universal. As Wendell Willkie puts it, there is "one world"—one physical neighborhood in which all the nations, races and classes have been thrown. But—and herein lies the crisis—we bring to this one world not a greatness and unity of spirit but a narrow provincialism. Our minds are filled with partialisms, while the physical forces of our culture are demanding and creating universalism. We cannot run a great society without greatness of spirit. We must have great conceptions, great imaginations, great emotions, great programs. We can't run a super-power dynamo with the steam from a teakettle.

There are two alternatives, and only two, before us. First, which is unlikely, is that we unscramble our modern interdependent culture, returning to separate and isolationist lives. If we went back to the village stage of existence, then we might be partialists to our hearts' content. Such a world would not *demand* greatness.

The other alternative is to so expand our spiritual powers that we vastly increase the range of our understanding and sympathy. There is no middle way. It is greatness—universalism—or perish.

There is no experience which gives to man so compelling a universalism as this radical religious insight into the unities and universals.

Notes

1. Italics mine, not Dr. Hocking's.
2. *What Man Can Make of Man*. By William Ernest Hocking. Harper's, New York, 1942.
3. *Journal Intime*. By Henri Frederic Amiel, Introduction.
4. Idem.
5. *Modern Man's Worship*. By Bernard Eugene Meland. p. 296. Harper and Brothers, 1934.
6. *Cosmic Religion*. By Albert Einstein. p. 48. Covici Friede, 1931. Italics are the author's.

"Superstition, Reason, and Faith" was the annual Russell Lecture at Tufts, delivered by Skinner in 1946 at the time of his retirement. He chose to return to the defense of liberal theology, centering on the relation of science to religion. As old belief systems break down, religion must be re-created in every generation. Superstitions continue to arise. He insists on the importance of reason, especially in religion. "To us moderns there are no closed systems in the heavens or on the earth. All is in flux, and we must apply the law of evolution to all religious tenets." Faith, he says, is "that force which carries belief into action. It is conviction plus courage." He concludes, "The only question for us is—will our faith be intelligent, or will it be obscured by superstition? . . . Shall faith be emancipated from the entanglements of the past so that it may greatly serve the present?" The lecture was published in The Christian Leader, *November 16 and December 7, 1946, and later distributed as a pamphlet.—JDH*

Superstition, Reason, and Faith

"The crisis of our age," says Prof. [Pitrim A.] Sorokin of Harvard University, "is marked by an extraordinary explosion of wars, revolutions, anarchy, and bloodshed; by social, moral, economic, political and intellectual chaos; by a resurgence of revolting cruelty and animality, and a temporary destruction of the great and small values of mankind; by misery and suffering on the part of millions—a convulsion far in excess of the chaos and disorganization of the ordinary crises."[1]

To live in such a time is stimulating, for it compels us to put a sharp edge to our capacity to think clearly and to feel profoundly. Such a period, however, is primarily one of bewilderment. We are conscious of a tremendous stir, but to what end? We know that we are being rushed along the stream of history, but where is our goal? Old systems and meanings are breaking down. Ruthlessly the world is discarding what the past treasured as stable values. Where are the new truths to take the place of the old? If our ancient good has become uncouth, where is the new good to take its place and sustain our spirits?

These questions, perhaps not always consciously formulated, are in the minds of many millions throughout the world. The post-war mood is one of wondering and groping. For half a century, we have been destroying values. The two world wars merely accentuated the process. But man does not live by negations alone. The soul craves some North Star by which it can set its course, some authoritative criterion of values in which it can put its confidence. Where shall the soul find such assurances, where shall it find firm foundations not built on the shifting sands of uncertitude, but on the solid rock of enduring reality?

Naturally we turn to religion for answer, since religion has traditionally given us the sense of permanence in the midst of change and of good in the midst of evil. It has been like the shadow of a mighty rock in a dry and desert land, like a well of water springing up within, to quench eternal thirst.

Many millions, however, cannot find the answer in the established religious systems because they do not seem to ring true to their method of thinking or to their fundamental beliefs. We have rejected many of the old theological doctrines as moribund, and have failed to create a vital religion to replace them. Lewis Mumford in his "Faith For Living" says, "The Twentieth Century inherited a morality which it never worked for, which it had never examined and criticized and assimilated, which it was incapable of reproducing in fresh forms that could be handed on to its children. The husk of religion remained but the precious life in its germ lacked a soil in which it could grow. Religion ceased gradually to be a social force and became a private idiosyncrasy."[2]

The Twentieth Century has been living on the unearned increment of religion and making few vital contributions to its renewal. We have been spending our spiritual capital at an alarming rate, so there need be no surprise if now, when we so desperately need that capital, we find it exhausted. We have assumed that life's highest values were stable goods. They were taken for granted as something "given" like earth and sky. They were simply there and all man had to do was to appropriate them. We now see the tragic mistake we have made. Religion and morality are not like the air we breathe, self-purifying and free. They must be recreated in every generation, and newly made part of our inner selves. To merely discard the old is not enough, for that leaves us living in a vacuum. We must create the new if we are to find abiding satisfaction.

Another reason why religion fails so many today is just the opposite from the reason given above. While some revolted and discarded the olden superstitions, others did not have the courage to do so, the result being that their religion became unreal and thus incapable of serving them in their hour of need. The orthodox systems of the traditional churches were so weighed down with superstition that they simply could not meet the minds of the desperate multitudes.

Religious leaders as a rule have been dominated by a desire to be helpful. They are pre-eminently men of good will and compassionate disposition, so they are under constant temptation to sacrifice truth for kindness. Knowing that Biblical lore is rich in emotional overtones, they continue using superstitions of the age of mythology, rather than drawing upon the materials of the present day which could stand a rational scrutiny. In this connection we must remember the stinging words of John Tyndall, "It is perfectly possible for you and me to purchase intellectual peace at the price of intellectual death."

Superstition

Let us now briefly define superstition, glance at its causes and see why it lingers in our religious life. The Oxford Dictionary defines the word as "Survival of old religious habit in the midst of a new order of things," "unreasoning awe or fear of something unknown, mysterious, or imaginary," "irrational or unfounded belief in general," "a tenet, scruple, habit, etc., founded on fear or ignorance."

The reason why superstition flourishes is easy to understand. Man is always obsolete. He never brings his mind completely alongside all events and discoveries, for he is too preoccupied. He simply cannot keep up to date in every field of knowledge for his brain cells are not adequate for such a superhuman task. He must lag behind complete contemporaneity. The result is superstition, which by derivation means "a remaining over."

Superstition flourishes most flagrantly in areas where either one of two conditions exist; namely, a) in matters which concern man most vitally, and b) in fields where precision measurements have not yet been invented or accepted. It reaches its apex when both of these conditions exist together. Like any broad generalization applying to social conditions, there are exceptions to the rule, but I believe that it will stand the test of scrutiny. A more detailed explanation of this statement follows.

a) When carefully analyzed it will be seen that most of our widely distributed myths and folklore have to do with important crises and interests. They arise from the will to believe, desire for security, hope of success in love, birth, adventure, conflict, and safe journey into immortality. Superstitions are rife in all fields where these values are supreme.

To touch upon only one field outside religion, we see that superstitions about health are among the most persistent. The history of medical and pseudomedical practice is full of witch-doctoring, plant signatures, magic herbs gathered at the right phase of the moon, divine beds, absorbing another's vitality, demon possession, exorcising and other forms of charlatanry too numerous to mention.[3]

Such ideas and practices are still in vogue through large portions of the world among peasants, mountaineers, and others who live in areas where modern culture has not penetrated. Such folk honestly believe in luck charms, witch's brews and weird concoctions, incantations and saint's bones, because they have a strong will to believe in anything that will promise health. The famous shrines of many religions testify to the healing power of Buddha's tooth or a saint's lock of hair. They believe in signs of the zodiac, animal augury, mis-shaped plants and a host of other superstitions about the prevention and cure of disease. The reason is not far to seek. Health is one of the basic and desired goods. The need for it is overwhelming. When robbed of it men will go to any extreme of belief or action to attain it. So, superstitions flourish.

This same statement holds regarding religions, for religion deals with the vital, intimate concerns of men. Aside from the cosmological aspect of religion which satisfies the craving to explain life, we have the so-called practical aspect of religion which deals with such concerns as sin and salvation.

Man has always felt that he is not a totally independent creature, free to act in defiance of powers of the universe greater than himself. He has felt that his destiny is in the hands of fate, mana, God, evil or good spirits. This insight is, of course, essentially sound, since everything we know about modern science reinforces man's primitive belief that he is a creature of the universe. Religion, then, deals with the great concerns which touch every individual at the deepest point in his life. But here we have illustrated the second condition which makes for superstition. Namely, b) the impossibility of applying exact measures and absolute scientific methods. Here is an area where precise definition cannot be applied. We cannot be entirely objective for the object is also the subject. Here the overpowering "will to believe" interferes with detached rationality. To use, for instance, the old theological terms, we want to be "saved." Despite shifting theological meanings we still want to be saved, by which we mean that we want spiritual security, peace of mind, adjustment to life, and happiness. Though sin is no longer a popular topic for sermons it is still a fact; witness war, drug addiction, sexualism, alcoholism, and crime. We want to escape these sins even if we call them by the innocent name of "complexes" of "neuroses."

We still fear death and we want to know what destiny has in store for us when our bodies return to the earth. Is it oblivion or is it immortality? Is it suffering or fulfillment? What is the meaning of life? Is there purpose in it or only blind drift?

These questions do not down, no matter whether we live in the African jungle, or on Michigan Boulevard. We are human, whether we are primitive or modern. We have the same fundamental urgencies, the same hopes and fears as our ancestors had. It is not strange then, that we possess a powerful will to believe and that we still cling to superstitions.

Most of the popular myths which persist in our time were formed in days when skepticism was not an organized form of culture and to doubt was not an intellectual requirement. To be naive was a common trait for no one feared that a psychoanalyst was lurking in the audience during conversation. They uttered their hopes and fears freely. They did not hesitate to reveal their inmost emotions. There was no sharp dividing line between poetic imagination and literal truth, so the religious traditions coming down from early history were a combination of naive credulity and profound insight, of primitive simplicity and the "deep dark wisdom of the soul." These beliefs were symbols which we have taken for signs.

Today our contemporary Judaism and Christianity are full of myths from Babylonia, Assyria, Egypt, Persia, Greece and Rome. They still retain anthropomorphisms and concretions which we must either reject because we cannot believe them to be true, or which we may retain because of historicity but which then become unreal and thus incapable of directing and moulding life.

Reason

If we are to rescue religion from the many incrustations of superstition we must focus upon it all the resources of reason which we possess; reason which is both analytical and creative, inductive and deductive, practical and theoretical. Religion cannot be a vital part of our lives unless we believe in it, and we cannot believe in it if it teaches what is contrary to the best and the truest that we know.

Religion is more than reason—far more, because it involves the whole man living in the whole universe. But since living involves definitive interpretations, we must be intelligent about what we believe. Thomas Huxley once wrote to his friend Kingsley: "I have searched over the grounds of my belief, and if wife and child and name and fame were all to be lost to me one after the other as the penalty, I will not lie. The longer I live, the more obvious it is to me that the most sacred act of a man's life is to say and to feel, 'I believe such and such to be true.' All the greatest rewards and all the heaviest penalties of existence cling about that act."[4] This should be a solemn exhortation to us all to realize that it matters tremendously both to ourselves and to the world that what we believe about important matters should be held only after we have honestly tried to arrive at the truth, the whole truth, and nothing but the truth.

There is no heresy greater than that which says, "Oh well, it doesn't matter what I believe." It *does* matter; it matters supremely whether we believe in good or evil, truth or lie, cruelty or kindness, freedom, tolerance or bigotry. The ethics of belief have been too much neglected. It is high time that we recognize the necessity of overhauling our beliefs for, as Emerson said, "What is inmost will in due time become outmost." Our convictions tend toward action. It is evil to believe a lie because we are apt to follow that belief by living a lie.

What then is reason? It is the "power or faculty of comprehending or inferring," "that intellectual power or faculty which is ordinarily employed in adapting thought or action to some end," "the guiding principle of the human mind in the process of thinking."

Without reason the universe would seem to us a hopeless jumble. Ideas, sense impressions, emotions would be a meaningless confusion. Without reason we could not conceive life systematically or bring meaning out of chaos. It is reason which gives significance and continuity to ideas. It alone accounts for our being able to see relationship between events and facts. Reason puts isolated impressions into their place and makes it possible to form schemes, and generalizations which are later to be tested as far as possible by controlled conditions.

To make a very homespun illustration, imagine that a native from Zanzibar is attending a football game. He sees thousands of folk waving colored flags, roaring and singing. He watches the crowds jump in glee and slump in despair. On the field he sees twenty or thirty huskies who seem to be sane, rushing pell mell at each other, throwing their arms and legs about promiscuously and slavishly following the skin of a pig. This may be civilization, says the Zanzabarian, but it isn't sense.

From the point of view of the man who has no key pattern in his mind, it isn't sense; but when he has achieved some "reason" for it all, he sees that this apparent meaningless chaos does follow certain rules, it has purpose and meaning.

This parable is meant to represent the function of reason in the apparent welter and jumble of undisciplined impressions and ideas which swarm through our minds. The mental life is like a tropical jungle, teaming with wild life, common, exotic, poisonous, medicinal—all luxuriant. Sense impressions crowd upon us from a rich and varied universe. Colors, forms, sounds, to the unreasoning mind are like the football game to the uninitiated. They are atomistic without form and void. By reason we endow fact and events with significance. We begin to generalize. We look inside ourselves and begin to separate the mental jungle growth into definite categories. That is the function of reason. It makes connections, pulls together apparently unrelated concretions, makes laws. It tries to trace a relation of cause and effect and thus establish dependability. It presides over empirical experimentation.

Reason has an especially important function to perform in religion, for the religious emotions such as awe and the sense of mystery are apt to be vague. The vastness and universality of their scope lend themselves to formlessness. The utter commitment of religion goes beyond the prudential thus making a clear definition of ends especially necessary. The glory of religion is that it seeks the unseen and unknown, but what is virtue under certain conditions of restraint and understanding may easily become vice under conditions of unrestraint and unguided emotionalism. Religious emotions are not wrong, but they must be made to serve the whole life and not be allowed to become ends in themselves.

Reason ties into a nexus of relationship all facts and forces. It unlocks the mystery of life with the key of meaning.

If religion is to be meaningful and vital it must be related to the knowledge and experiences common to men. It must be integrated into morals, art and science as we know them. It must be brought up to date so that it squares with our concept of reality. A god who is tribal, has favorites, reproduces children by human mothers, sets aside the laws of the universe and is otherwise provincial and fickle is unbelievable in view of what is common knowledge today. Yet much of the theology and ritual of our churches harks back to the days when that kind of god was acceptable to the minds of men. Our religious literature is full of superstition; literally, that which is left over from another age.

When men believed in a closed universe, as they did in the Middle Ages, it was logical to believe in a closed revelation of truth and in a closed system of theology. It was not unreasonable; that is, out of harmony with the general outlook, to accept the static view. The effect upon the present and future, however, has been tragic for it was largely responsible for freezing ancient myths into the system of Christian theology. So deep rooted are they now that it seems sacrilege to many to pull them up and to relegate them to the museum where we keep relics.

Today we must accept the dynamic contact of life. To us moderns there are no closed systems in the heavens or on the earth. All is in flux and we must apply the law of evolution to all religious tenets. God, revelation, saviour and salvation must be interpreted as changing with a developing universe. Nothing is finished, not even God. The Bible is a continuing library. Christ is one of a long line of redeemers. Christian theology is not final or absolute, but is to be added to, subtracted from, and developed in the light of what we shall learn in the future.

Reason has an enormous task to perform in opening the closed doors of religion so that it may look out upon the world as it is. To many of those who are desperately anxious to conserve the high values of Christianity, a radical discarding of Christian mythology would seem extremely dangerous. If we begin so daring a task when and where shall we stop? Shall we not eventually destroy the whole system? Far from it. Those who have the courage to discard the unbelievable are the ones who are conserving the precious truth at the heart of Christianity. Those who insist upon retaining the incredible are the ones who will make Christianity eventually so unreal as to cause the entire system to be discredited. The keepers of the Greek and Roman religion were unwilling to let go ancient mythology long after the people had ceased to believe in it. The result was death. Let us remember that lesson!

In this hour of the world's greatest crisis, the need for a living, transforming Christianity is frighteningly urgent. High destiny or doom waits upon our fateful decision. Shall we free Christianity from the encumbrances which crush its spirit?

Prof. [John] Dewey says, "The issue does not concern this and that piecemeal item of belief, but centers in the question of the method by which any and every item of intellectual belief is to be arrived at and justified. The significant bearing, for my purpose in all this is that new methods of inquiry and reflection have become for the educated man today the final arbiter of all questions of fact, existence, and intellectual assent. Nothing less than a revolution in the 'seat of intellectual authority' has taken place. This revolution, rather than any particular aspect of its impact upon this and that religious belief, is the central thing. The mind of man is being habituated to a new method and ideal. There is but one sure road of access to truth—the road of patient, co-operative inquiry operating by means of observation, experiment, record and controlled reflection."[5]

Who can doubt that these words are a challenge which Christianity must accept or resign itself to increasing impotence?

But all is not plain sailing for those who would embark upon a revolutionary appraisal of Christianity's assets and liabilities.

Today there is a strong move against trusting in reason which arises chiefly from three sources.

First, there is resistance from those who would have us return to a primitive animalism, stressing the unconscious bodily drives. "There is an uprising of the darker and less familiar inhabitants of the underworld against an intellectualism that had regarded itself as supreme."[6] It represents a dialectic swing away from the inadequacies of the enlightenment. D. H. Lawrence represents this school of thought, or rather feeling, when he writes, "My great religion is a belief in the blood, the flesh, as being wiser than the intellect. We can go wrong in our minds. But what our blood feels, and believes, and says, is always true."[7] The racialism of the Nazi movement was one logical outcome of such a revolt against rationality.

Secondly, we find many scientists attacking rationalism on grounds that empirical knowledge is alone safe. We must experiment and submit to controlled experience. It is not enough to use our reason. We must employ the test tube and at every possible step in the experiment, check and recheck.

Reason must be held in restraint, else it may lead us into a world which is mere idea. Scientific opposition to speculative reason is specially strong. There are many who would deny its validity, thus banning philosophy and all its works. Of them Prof. [Alfred North] Whitehead says, "Obscurantism is the refusal to speculate freely on the limitations of traditional methods. It is more than that; it is the negation of the importance of such speculation, the insistence on incidental dangers. A few generations ago the clergy, or to speak more accurately, large sections of the clergy, were the standing examples of obscurantist. Today their place has been taken by scientists—

'By merit raised to that bad eminence.'

The obscurantists of any generation are in the main constituted by the greater part of the practitioners of the dominant methodology. Today scientific methods are dominant, and scientists are the obscurantists."[8]

What Whitehead is here protesting against is not science nor scientists as such, but those who put a narrow limitation upon man's search for meaning and value. A limited methodology is a denial of the right of the whole of human nature to embark upon "the research magnificent." No one instrumentality can give us the whole truth about the whole of life. The empirical method must embrace reason and faith, just as faith must embrace empiricism and reason.

The third group consists of those religionists who wish to defend their ancient creed from the assaults of logic. They fall back on fear and the craving for security. They cannot face the possibility of their system being disintegrated, for their spiritual lives are at stake. So they retreat into impervious defenses and proclaim that religion is founded on something deeper and more valid than reason. Karl Barth in an example of this group. He "defends an uncompromising transcendentalism, more extreme than that of Neo-Platonism or Augustine. God is supreme Sovereign of the world, who speaks to man in his Word (the Bible) but who is entirely *separated from and discon-*

tinuous with human thought and experience."[9]

In such a brief essay as this, it is impossible to treat these three sources of anti-intellectualism with more than these few passing words. We must realize, however, that each group has some elements of truth and we must therefore realize that rationality has its limits.

Faith

It is a truism to say that we do not live to think, but that we think to live. Reason is not the single goal, the end all of the evolutionary process. It is one of the means toward progress. It is far from perfect; it may mislead, be misused and it frequently contradicts itself. Reason, therefore, must be considered as a part of the whole man. It should be recognized as one of the many endowments of a pluralistic human nature. It must be subordinated to team work; cooperating with primitive drives, insight or intuition, experience, common sense, habit and faith. Only under those conditions can it be fully trusted.

When reason becomes isolated, it runs into a dead end. It is quite possible to philosophize one's self out of existence. By reasoning apart from life's urgencies, one can achieve an almost complete skepticism which denies reality and value to everything including reason and the person who reasons. This, of course, is a perversion of nature for it is nature's command that we have at least an animal belief in the actualities of existence, and that, like other animals, we have the courage to put that belief into action, which is faith.

We must go beyond rationality, since it can be both erratic and limited. That does not mean that we should discard it, far from it. We must exploit all its resources, but if we are to know the fullness of life we must go with faith beyond the limits of reason. I have said that man does not live by negations alone, and that is true. Negations sometimes must be made, however, such as eliminating error and superstition. But eventually we must seek positive ideas and ideals. We must set out upon an adventure towards those truths men live by, and that is supremely the task of faith.

What, then, is faith? I shall define it as that force which carries belief into action. It is conviction plus courage. It is the dynamic power which urges us to put our philosophy to the test of experience. "Faith," writes Prof. [Nils] Ferré, "is a matter of total positive commitment and basic affirmative attitudes."[10] Faith is not necessarily irrational or anti-rational. It springs from something deeply implanted in human nature; namely, the impulse to action, to go beyond the limitations of the seen and provable into the realm of the unseen and unproved.

There have been periods when faith meant the antithesis of reason, something which descended from above by supernatural means, or something which we must believe on command from the proper authority. In this sense faith was identical with a submissive acceptance. The individual concerned bowed to the august sanction of some divine power, or to the superior intelligence or prestige of someone in high position. Or the conviction might arise from the prompting of some inner intuition or mystic experience. In any case, instead of wrestling over the matter, examining it from every possible angle, integrating it into one's general background and frame of reference, he surrendered his privilege of applying logic to the problem. He decided that "It is not mine to reason why. Better men than I have told me that the case must be so and so." Or perhaps he said, "I know that this is so because something inside me compels me to believe it."

During such periods it was considered a virtue to have faith in the sense of an uncritical acceptance of a dogma. It showed an especially religious nature to be willing to submit to authority.

At the present time, however, the meaning of faith has been undergoing an evolution. There is a widespread movement to define it, not in terms of submissive acceptance but rather in terms of an active, organic self-giving to something believed.

We are coming to think of faith as a "whole response" to a whole situation. It includes body, mind and soul. It does not discard authority, but makes obedience to authority a part of the whole act of the whole personality. This view is supported by such well-known writers as Dewey, Wieman, Fosdick, Ferré, and others. If this view is accepted, it will be seen that faith implies reason rather than setting up an antithesis to it.

Another meaning of faith current in former times made it equivalent to sectarian creed, such as Jewish, Catholic, or Protestant. But this becomes untenable if we accept the newer meaning outlined above. There are sectarian creeds in the sense that each religious group emphasizes certain tenets, or distinctive doctrines. But faith is something much more comprehensive than speculative belief. It is common to all religions. Creed is sectarian, faith is human. Creed is what we believe, faith is the act of will which puts the belief into action.

John Cowper Powys, the brilliant English essayist, speaks of fish which frequently leap from the water into the air. We are so accustomed to this phenomenon that we rarely ponder its significance. Here is an animal with limited sensory equipment, with reasoning powers of the lowest order, if any; an animal born in and adjusted to the water. His whole life function is confined to this element; he breathes, finds food, reproduces, swims, rests in the water. In the nature of the case, such an animal can know nothing of the air. He cannot know that there is any existence outside that within which he moves and has his being. Yet a great many species of fish leap out of their known world into the unseen air. They cannot know whether they will be burned or frozen or how they will fare in this totally foreign element. Yet they make the leap.

All analogies break down at some point, and I would not want to press this one for its limitations are so obvious that it can hardly be called an analogy. It is, rather, a striking figure of speech which makes it possible for us to visualize the meaning of faith.

Prof. [George] Santayana has pointed out that we humans

are physiologically born in and adjusted to a certain physical environment consisting of known and very limited elements. We survive as organisms when we are harmoniously adjusted to these known and describable conditions. We have no knowledge of any other world. We move, live, and have our being, worry, have arthritis, grow bald, and die here on this limited planet. But something strange stirs within our imagination. We dream of worlds that must ever be beyond our mortal ken. There are those who believe that there are planes of living as different from ours as air is from water. Even the hard-headed Herbert Spencer said that as a dog has no consciousness of what lies behind the book covers in his master's library, so we humans may be living in a universe of significance and meaning which we never glimpse through reason or sense but faith points to as real. Evelyn Underhill speaks of our "rich and many leveled environment," implying that we who live in a three-dimensional world have not necessarily exhausted all the possibilities of existence.

To return to Prof. Santayana, after pointing out that man never seems satisfied with physical conditions even when they are at their very best, he goes on to say that this is so because "things seen are temporal and things unseen are eternal." Certain it is that merely being well-fed and satisfied with all the wealth of the physical world does not give man the "abiding satisfactions."

What, then, lies "out there" in the universe beyond the comprehension of even our most sensitively perceptive personalities? We do not know. Superstition peoples that vast unknown with powers and entities which we of this enlightened age must doubt or deny.

The reports which reason brings from its investigation are conflicting but certainly astounding. Science reveals potentialities in the world of today which go beyond the dreams of the Nineteenth Century. But reason can go so far and no further.

Yet the lure of the unknown and the ideal cause us to strain at limitations as the imprisoned bird tries to break from his cage, or as the fish gathers strength for that epochal leap from the known element into the unknown. By faith we send our vision beyond the actual and the seen into the realm of what may be the profoundly real. And as Prof. James was fond of asserting, faith helps to make what seems impossible to become possible.

We must recognize that faith, like courage, does not always nicely discriminate between potentialities that are right and wrong. It takes the raw material which conviction provides and uses it. Faith may be just as powerful a force for evil as for good, it may act just as vigorously on the basis of error as of truth. It may utilize superstition or obscurantist doctrine as well as the proved law of science. Its fires utilize any and every kind of fuel, hate as well as love.

Some concrete examples will clarify this point. At regular intervals throughout history, the doctrine of the end of the world is revived, and thousands of people implicitly believe it. This doctrine is founded on the idea of the cataclysmic character of both physical and social nature. Just as there are earthquakes and terrible fires, so human history is marked by the cataclysms of wars and plagues. Someday, according to the end-of-the-world philosophy, lightning will flash and thunder roar, quakes will shake the earth, the "terror that walketh at noon day" will stalk abroad;—all the horrors that man has ever known will visit this unhappy earth. Then the trumpet will sound, graves will give up the dead, some will rise to eternal bliss, others will sink to endless torment. The end of the world will come with the suddenness of a clap of thunder.

Many people believe this, but do nothing about it, letting prudence be the better part of valor. They will wait and see. Some have faith in it, which means that they have a tendency to put their belief to the test of action. They give away their homes, their bank accounts, even their war bonds. They hie them to the roof tops, clad in sheets, to welcome the dawn and to be a little nearer heaven. There they wait the crack of doom which does not crack. Finally, cold and disillusioned, they come back to unregenerate earth to beg a cup of coffee from those stiff-necked scoffers who had no faith.

On the contrary, there are those who hold to the evolutionary theory regarding both the physical and social nature of man. Such persons believe that the end of this planet will result from a gradual cooling process, taking millions of years. Social institutions will evolve by a process of willed adaptation and historic continuity. Those who have faith in this scheme of things live as if it were true. They plan their lives as if there would be a solid earth under their feet and some sort of social stability which we can count on.

Both groups are betting their lives on their belief. Neither one knows. Our planet may be hit by a comet, or more terrible wars may destroy our institutions. It is a matter of faith. In both cases, there has been both reason and faith, but neither has necessarily been infallible.

The situation is clearly put by Prof. Ferré: "Faith's total context of meaning cannot by its very nature be wholly validated because as yet it is not. The actual is what it is and can be roughly tested or experienced as such. The ideal, however, is so exceptionally and fragmentarily realized, especially as it approaches its fullness, that only an act of faith can designate it with assurance as ultimate reality."[11] There is the problem in a nut shell. It states both the advantages and the disadvantages of faith.

Faith, like reason, may go wrong, but it may also go magnificently right. On the side of its constructive triumphs Paul lists some of the great victories of the Hebrews, such as those of Abraham and Moses in establishing the faith and homeland of the Jews. He goes on in a sweeping description of "all those who through faith subdued kingdoms, wrought righteousness, obtained promises, stopped the mouth of lions, quenched the power of fire, escaped the edge of the sword, from weakness were made strong." We might extend the list to modern times by including the Pilgrims, the scientists, the social workers, reformers, educators, physicians and many others.

Whenever man has triumphed over apparently insuperable obstacles, wherever he has wrung secrets from the unknown, wherever he has achieved the ideal, there and then he has employed faith.

Faith is the greatest creative force in the history of man. Without it no movement can go forward to peace or righteousness. Faith awakens the constructive powers of men. It fills them with the courage to dare and to do. It turns potentialities into actualities. It sees under the unpromising exterior of things a seed of promise and hope. Faith sees a free man in a slave, a reformed man in a criminal, a decent world in the midst of ravaging war. If we are ever to rebuild this shattered old world, we must have faith.

Religious faith has traditionally removed mountains because it is backed by the greatest power in the world—the infinite. There is only one force potentially greater than the energy released from the atom, and that is faith that man shall control that energy and turn it to constructive good.

There is no question as to whether man is going to bring faith to bear upon the present great crisis in the world's culture. We cannot fail to utilize faith, for faith is a tendency to action, and man is ineradicably a creation of action. Our reasons and our emotions seek and will find overt expression. The only question for us is—will our faith be intelligent, or will it be obscured by superstition? Will it be directed toward desired ends, or will it be directed toward futility? Will it be motivated by ideas which are credible or incredible? Shall faith be emancipated from the entanglements of the past so that it may greatly serve the present?

We must not isolate any instrumentality which can possibly be used for discovering the meaning and value of life. All the means which we possess must be employed in the co-operative adventure against the realms of ignorance and evil.

May I suggest that the religious ideal at its best is:—

The whole life
of the whole personality
in the whole of the universe.

In closing this essay, I want to emphasize the fact that I have not tried to solve all the problems of religion. I have merely tried to throw some light upon some of its problems, and to suggest lines of approach. Nothing could be more fitting than to quote as my last words a beautiful passage by Gilbert Murray—

"The Uncharted surrounds on every side, and we needs must have some relation to it, a relation which will depend on the general discipline of a man's mind and the bias of his whole character. As far as knowledge and conscious reason will go, we should follow resolutely their austere guidance. When they cease, as cease they must, we must use as best we can those fainter powers of apprehension and surmise and sensitivity by which, after all, most high truth has been reached as well as most high art and poetry; careful always really to seek for truth and not for our own emotional satisfaction, careful not to neglect the real needs of men and women through basing our lives on dreams; and remembering above all, to walk gently in a world where the lights are dim and the very stars wander."[12]

Notes

1. "The Crisis at Our Age" by P. A. Sorokin, E. P. Dutton & Co. 1942, p. 22.
2. "Religion for Free Minds" by Lewis Mumford, Harcourt Brace Co., pp. 20-21.
3. See "Devils, Drugs and Doctors."
4. "Life and Letters" of Thomas H. Huxley.
5. "A Common Faith" by John Dewey, Yale University Press, p. 32.
6. "Religion for Free Minds" by Julius S. Bixler, Harper Bros., 1939, p. 43.

7. "The Letters of D.H. Lawrence," Viking Press, 1932.
8. "Function of Reason" by Alfred N. Whitehead, Princeton Univ.
9. "Types of Religious Philosophy" by Edwin Burtt, Harper, p. 434.
10. "Reason and Faith" by Nils Ferré, Harper and Bros., 1946, p. 23.
11. Ibid., p. 225.
12. "Five Stages of Greek Religion" by Gilbert Murray, Columbia Univ. Press.

What Is Worship?

One who writes on so intimate and elusive a subject as worship must steer between the Sahara of barren definition and the flood of fulsome emotion.

On the one hand, dictionaries give us prosaic words which fail to transmit the fire and warmth of religious experience as completely as the chemical formula of a diamond fails to describe the brilliant flash of colors which are in the heart of that precious stone. Reality is infinitely more important than its explanation. Dictionaries give us truth, but they do not give us reality. Worship is an experience, moving and colorful. It is an act involving the emotional life and as such transcends explanation. It is reality, and no words "about it and about" can change that basic fact. No arid intellectualism can be substituted for the glowing experience. When we are hungry no chemical formula can take the place of bread. We want substance, not words. Likewise, the hunger of the soul cannot be satisfied by a definition. That religion which is experiential transcends all commentaries. It is authentic and real. The rationalism of the late nineteenth century failed to satisfy the deepest needs of the human spirit, so the twentieth century shifts its emphasis from critical dissection to living experience.

On the other hand, if we merely revel in undisciplined and undefined emotion we can have no clear idea of the significance and worth of the thing we experience, and we can have no common understanding of the subject which we are discussing. We humans are under bonds to be intelligent about what we do and feel. We are by nature reflective, and no normal person can merely watch the stream of life flow by him without wanting to understand its meaning. To experience religion is good, but what about its validity and worth? As Prof. [John] Dewey has pointed out, we can experience insanity, but that does not make it desirable. We experience war with all its horrors, and we feel its reality with an indescribable urgency, but that does not excuse us from the moral and intellectual responsibility of clearly defining the issues involved. So with worship. We are compelled to ask: What does this particular experience signify? What is its nature? How does it fit into the frame of reference which is ours at any one time in history?

Somewhere between the two extremes of arid intellectualism and fulsome emotionalism we may find an understanding of worship. We need both the cold clarity of definition and the warmth of full-blooded experience to make reality.

If this subject is to be considered analytically and scientifically, it must be removed from the exclusive realm of theology where it has been enveloped with an aura of mysticism. It should be placed in the category of history and psychology where it can be studied by the secular mind without presuppositions. It must be thought of as a form of human behavior as old as the human race and as ubiquitous.

We cannot ignore history, and the record of man's religious interests shows that worship has often been directed toward a multiplicity of objects other than God. There are holy mountains in China and Japan, lofty peaks towering toward Heaven, which are prayed to by millions of the devout. There are great rivers running through continents of the Orient which are thought of as dispensers of fertility and are prayed to as sources of life and prosperity. There are sun, moon, and stars, winds and storms, which have been the objects of reverence in many cultures. There are heroes, saints, and holy men, even buildings and man-made symbols before which worshippers have knelt in supplication, awe or hope. There were Druids of old who worshipped visible forms of nature, and there are fire-worshippers who still perform religious rites before a holy flame. Surely, in view of history's records we cannot narrow our study of this problem to one particular form—that which implies a Deity.

Let us recognize that worship is not an esoteric act separated from all other human concerns by an unbridgeable chasm called *mysticism*, or *other-worldliness*. It is not divine in the sense of contrast to being human. It springs from the same root as many other experiences, and shares with them common motives and methods. It is a natural phenomenon and need not involve any supernaturalism. It can be explained by the same laws which explain other forms of human behavior. It is a phase of human nature, somewhat akin to art, music or poetry, and even to some phases of adventure and science. It has a wider meaning than that which modern ecclesiasticism has assigned to it.

Worship exists wherever there is tension between the individual and an object which he reverently holds to be of highest significance and value. It is the outreach of man to attain union with this object—to know it, to feel it, to experience it. The word worship has a strictly religious connotation, but it need not necessarily be so.

Worship preceded a religion, or any of its formal rites and ceremonies, even theological ideas. Certainly worship must have existed long before the concept of God dawned upon the mind of man, and it can exist today where God is not an active idea force. Nature, beauty, great men, or truth may be worshipped. When God becomes the object, no new mental process is invented or brought into play. There is simply a new orientation which directs man's outreach toward a new object.

The content or object of this experience is not the chief consideration, although it is important. The significant fact is that worship is a natural form of behavior for all people. Wherever there is a tension between the actual and the ideal, and wherever there is a reverent outreaching for the unattained—there is worship.

Let us briefly illustrate the universality of this naturalistic outreach in spheres which are not commonly thought of as distinctly religious.

A mountain climber may experience all the elements of worship if scaling a distant peak is to him an event of high significance and ulterior value. A dweller in the valley may look up to a snow-covered summit glistening against a blazing blue sky. The sight may awaken in him a sense of the sublime and he feels the call of the heights. Something beckons to his spirit to forsake the lowlands and climb the precipitous cliffs to the loftiest possible elevation. The physical act of struggling upward and catching glimpses of majestic spaces and wide horizons may symbolize some inner urgency and spiritual experience. He longs to make the ascent so that he may stand tip-toe on the summit of the world, wide-armed in welcome communion with infinity. Tension arises between himself as a consciously limited person dwelling in the valley, and an ideal of himself as a person enfranchised and enlarged by the noble experience of reaching the snow-shining summit surrounded by limitless space.

A lover may worship his beloved. Many an adolescent has thought of the object of his love as the embodiment of everything beautiful and good. The mist of romanticism has colored reality, endowed it with ideality, and set it at the end of a vista to be worshipped. So a poet may worship beauty, as well as a devout man may worship God. Psychologically, the experience is the same. The inner tension, the valuation and the outreach are all part of one common form of human behavior.

The musician feels the essential elements of worship when he strives to compose a great work of art. Beauty to him is "old yet ever new, eternal voice and inward word." It lays hold upon him with a sense of urgency, and haunts him until he can give form to its illusive spirit. Chords run through his soul, now almost grasped—now retreating, beckoning. The artist strives with his whole being to reach perfection, and to make it sing in a human throat or to throb in a violin.

Psychologically, this is worship. There is an object which, though immaterial, is authentic and real. There is a striving of the human mind toward that reality, and a commitment to its demands.

The same may be said of all the arts. A sensitive mind gropes toward an understanding of some significant truth. There is a yearning toward it, a consuming desire to lay hold of it, to body it forth in some almost perfect expression, word, color or shape.

A scientist may also feel this tension as he seeks to discover some new secret of nature, or to bring forth a new invention. Surely the lives of the Curies illustrate this fundamental trait as they gave everything in one dedicated pursuit of radium. The moment when these two devout souls first looked upon a glowing particle of the precious material shining in the darkness of their laboratory was filled with wonder and awe. There was as reverent a hush as when some worshipper looks upon the Eucharist. Here was one of the great moments in the history of man's struggle against ignorance and pain. Long sleepless nights, poverty, untiring search into the mysterious unknown was at last rewarded with a sense of triumph and accomplishment. Striving toward truth with all the strength of body and mind is like praying to God.

Sociologically, this experience may come to a reformer who strains with all his tense being toward the accomplishment of some great cause—perhaps the freeing of slaves, or the establishment of communism. The movement enlists his complete loyalty and calls for his unstinted commitments. In this something greater than self he sees an ultimate value which symbolizes for him justice and righteousness. Before it he stands humbled and exalted. By its victory he feels "disturbed by the joy of elevated thoughts." In its struggles he finds liberation from the mean and limited and union with what is great.

There is no essential difference between these experiences of the mountain climber, the lover, the artist, the scientist, and the reformer on one hand and the religionist on the other.

This wider interpretation is attested by common usage. [Thomas] Carlyle writes a lusty book to prove that hero worship is an innate form of human behavior. Whether the great man is poet, soldier, priest or sage, he is held in awe and reverence by the masses. The people look to him as an embodiment of some excellence and they worship him. Many sophisticated critics believed that in the twentieth century we would outgrow such adolescence, but they are being disillusioned by the facts. One of the astonishing manifestations of contemporary history is the renaissance of hero worship. The body of Lenin lies in pomp in his tomb in the Red Square, and endless lines of Russians file by to bow in hushed solemnity; and this in the Soviet which would minimize the importance of man and exalt economic determinism! The Mahatma (great soul) Gandhi was well on the way to becoming a Hindu incarnation, such was the spell he cast over millions of his devout followers. The fiery Hitler was adored by fanatic Nazis and was rapidly rising toward apotheosis when his system crumbled and his heroic stature shrank to common mold. Stalin, Mussolini, and others attest the tendency of man to worship something, if it is only himself in glorified form.

State-ism, with its garish display of flags, its goose-stepping ritual, its bloody sacrifices and its exaltation of "masse-Mensch" is at least partially caused by a frustration of the normal tendency to worship something noble. If that tendency is denied legitimate outlet, then it will turn to a pathological form. So deeply implanted in human nature is the need for worship that, like all other urgencies, it will seek an object, be it high or low, good or bad.

Dr. [Bernard] Meland asks, "Can this generation worship?" The answer is, we can do no other. We may not be able to worship the same objects as in the past, or to express our need in the traditional forms; but man is so made that he simply cannot escape the necessity of reaching, upward and outward toward something greater than himself. That something may be an unachieved ideal that beckons and urges him; it may be the summation of the sustaining forces of the universe; or, sad to say, it may be a brutal social order which exalts naked power. Whatever the unseen and distant goal, man never has lived a dreamless life, content to adjust his whole being to things as they are. The light that shines for him "never was on sea or land." For the vision splendid he will set in motion a million-footed army, he will fly in the air, and penetrate the infested swamps. Nothing seen or known can satisfy the hunger of our hearts and minds. In the dust that is man there shines an unearthly flame.

Worship is one of the essential elements in a normal, fully developed life. It springs from impulses planted deep in the psyche, and its practice corresponds to an urgent need. Worship is the craving for a reality which transcends our daily experience. It must never be forgotten that while man shares much of his nature with the animal, he differs from the animal in many fundamental respects. Man-in-culture yearns for something better than the actual. He idealizes, and is eternally building castles in Spain. He must look to something greater, better, more beautiful than he has ever known. It is only thus that he can grow and outgrow. Man has an insatiable thirst for the unattained. He is always and everywhere a pilgrim seeking a far country. He cannot remain satisfied with any embodiment of goodness or truth. Inexorably man is driven on toward unseen goals.

Let us now come to grips with the relation of worship to God. This is a specialized form of human behavior, which, as we have seen, is of universal significance. Ecclesiastical usage has made worship almost synonymous with the practice of the presence of God, and since that is what the word connotes in the minds of most people, we should analyze it in the light of that fact.

Our definition seems to hold when we change the so-called secular object such as beauty, truth or reform, to God. There is the subjective side—man, with his emotions of awe and reverence; there is the objective element—God, who is the symbol of all man's highest ideals; and there is the striving on the part of man to reach out toward God, "to feel after Him if happily we may find Him." There is an expansive impulse, a desire on the part of man to come into the presence of God, to know Him, to love Him, and to do His will.

The theologian insists that the worship of God differs in many important respects from that of a mountain, music, reform, or science. God represents the all-inclusive, the perfect, yet the loving and the human. All worship except the religious is particularistic and therefore partial. In the pursuit of perfection in music or poetry we are limited to one exclusive aspect of reality. We select out of an infinity of values only those which are of a special category. The artist may be insensitive to the glory of scientific truth or to the magnificent sweep of some great movement for human emancipation. The scientist may be absorbed in a microscopic cell, lost to a sense of beauty. The reformer may shut out from his view the entire cosmos and narrow his ideal to the arena of man. The mountain climber may have none of the tender and warm emotion of the lover. Each object of reverent expansiveness of soul thus carries with it a limitation which inheres in its very nature. God alone is all-embracing, and thus He alone is worthy of the highest type of worship. The theologian says God is the summation of all values, thus His worship contains no restrictions or imperfections. Other objects, being imperfect, sometimes fail; God, being perfection, never fails.

The majesty and all-mightiness of God transcend the towering Himalayas as the Universe is greater than the earth. An infinitude of space and an Eternity of time are His. If we take the wings of the morning and fly to the uttermost bounds of the sea, behold, He is there. If we sweep the Heavens with the telescope to a distance of a thousand light years, behold God! If we make our bed in the grave, we cannot escape His presence. Such knowledge is too wonderful for man. We fall to our knees overwhelmed with a sense of infinitude, and we worship.

The love and warmth of God transcend that of a woman as the Infinite transcends the finite. Not only is God all majesty and august power, but the theologian insists that by His incarnation in Christ He revealed Himself as the Father, compassionate, yearning to ingather all humanity into His great heart. In the worship of such a God man finds the warmth and glow of a divine affection. The human becomes divine, and the divine becomes human.

The scientist worships law as revealed in science, but God's law transcends that of man's discovery as the All rises above the fragmentary. God—the one all-inclusive unity and universality. God, the causal power, the Creator, the giver of law to the cosmos! To discover such a truth is to stand in silent awe of the Supreme revelation. Back of the discoveries of the marvels of science lies the marvel of God. If chemistry and physics are full of wonder and surprise, how much more so is worship, which lifts the eye of man to the source beyond science! If the created is wonderful how much more so is the Creator!

Thus the worship of God contains all the elements of all other worship experiences carried upward to perfection and infinity. It commands the whole psyche and calls for a complete dedication of spirit.

There are two facts, however, which must be stated in this connection: first, one can believe in God without experiencing what Carlyle called "transcendent wonder, wonder for which there is no limit or measure." One may believe in God as an abstract intellectual proposition in somewhat the same way as a mathematician believes in X. As we have said, man is under bonds to be intelligent and he wants to find a formula which explains the problem of existence. The author of the Book of Genesis sought an answer to the riddle of the universe, and he found it in the formula: "In the beginning, God!" So untold others have solved the continuing mystery of life by saying, "God!" Who was the author of creation? What is the unmoved mover and the uncaused cause? How can this vast galaxy of stars and these microscopic cells follow such inexorable law? The answer is—God! Millions can believe that, but the belief in and of itself does not necessarily imply an attitude of reverence or awe.

Secondly, it must be understood that one may even go through the motions of ecclesiastical liturgy, endlessly repeating the name of God, and still have no emotion of the august and sublime. A "good" member of the church may tell his beads in as purely mechanical a way as the bank teller reckons his day's transactions on the adding machine. The writer once sat next to a man who was kneeling in church, praying his "pater noster," while at frequent intervals he spat upon the floor. A repetition of the forms and rites of theism does not connote a genuine inward sense of devotion any more than hanging a strip of cloth printed with a prayer on a tree is a genuine prayer. One can go to the most magnificent cathedral on earth, partake in the communal recitation of great creeds without experiencing a moment's visitation of the divine fire. On the other hand, one's cup may be filled to overflowing while walking in the redwood forests of California or riding out a storm on the Atlantic.

Theology thus does not necessarily imply worship, and worship does not necessarily imply theology. The two things may properly go together, but they may be, and sometimes are, logically separated.

Bibliography

Alan Seaburg

This bibliography lists Skinner's published articles, books, pamphlet publications, and material written about his ideas and activities. It first appeared in the 1964-65 issue of *The Annual Journal* and has been updated for this volume.

BOOKS

The Social Implications of Universalism. Boston: Universalist Publishing House, 1915. (Reprinted in the *Annual Journal of the Universalist Historical Society*, 5:89-122, 1964-65; and by the Universalist Historical Society and Beacon Press as number 4 in the Beacon Reference Series, 1966, pp. 5-14.)

Liberalism Faces the Future. New York: Macmillan, 1937.

Human Nature and the Nature of Evil. Boston: Universalist Publishing House, 1939.

A Religion for Greatness. Boston: Murray, 1945. (Reprinted 1958.)

Worship and a Well Ordered Life. Boston: Universalist Historical Society and Meeting House Press, 1955.

BOOK WITH ANOTHER AUTHOR

_____ and Cole, Alfred S. *Hell's Ramparts Fell. The Life of John Murray.* Boston: Universalist Publishing House, 1941.

BOOK EDITED BY SKINNER

A Free Pulpit in Action. New York: Macmillan, 1931. ("Explanatory," pp. 1-17; "Shall the Citizens of Boston Be Allowed to Discuss Changing Their Laws?" a joint talk with Margaret Sanger and J. M. Landis; "What Constitutes a Healthy Mind?" pp. 197-218).

WRITINGS IN OTHER VOLUMES

Encyclopedia of Religion. Edited by Vergilius Ferm. New York: Philosophical Library, 1945. ("Hosea Ballou," p. 53; "Hosea Ballou 2nd," p. 53; "Alonzo Ames Miner," p. 492; "John Murray," p. 511; "Universalism," pp. 805-6.)

Levi Moore Powers. *A Memorial By His Friends.* Boston: Murray, 1921. ("Dr. Powers as Prophet," pp. 25-8.)

National Federation of Religious Liberals. 3d Congress. New York. 1911.

The Unity of Life. Philadelphia: The Federation, 1911. ("Remarks," pp. 44-5.) Tufts Papers on Religion.

A Symposium. Boston: Universalist Publishing House, 1939. ("What Religion Means to Me," pp. 7-16.)

Voices of Liberalism 2. Boston: Beacon Press, 1948. ("Superstition, Reason, and Faith," pp. 203-20.)

We Speak of Life. Edited by Vincent Silliman. Boston: Beacon Press, 1955. ("What Is Worship?," selection 41.)

At Thine Altar. Edited by Charles A. Wyman. Boston: Murray, 1946. ("The Secret Places of the Heart," p. 11; "For Kindliness," p. 13; "For a Universal Life," p. 14; "Facing Life," p. 16; "Forgive Our Foolish Ways," p. 17; "For Renewal," p. 18.)

ARTICLES IN PERIODICALS
(Listed in chronological order.)

"Consolation," *Universalist Leader*, n.s. 11 (March 28, 1908): 394.

"Why Not a Peace Day?," *Universalist Leader*, n.s. 13 (March 26, 1910): 401.

"Militarism or Christianity?," *Universalist Leader*, n.s. 14 (April 29, 1911): 526-8.

"Concerning the Peace Movement," *Universalist Leader*, n.s. 4 (October 14, 1911): 1295.

"Character or Conditions," *Universalist Leader*, n.s. 14 (December 16, 1911): 1597-8.

"Church and Channels for Action," *Survey*, 27 (January 13, 1912): 1588-9.

"A Reply to Mr. Briggs," *Universalist Leader*, n.s. 15 (February 3, 1912): 140.

"Social Service Commission," *Universalist Leader*, n.s. 15 (February 17, 1912): 210.

"Opportunities for Social Service," *Universalist Leader*, n.s. 15 (March 2, 1912): 272-4.

"Social Service Commission," *Universalist Leader*, n.s. 15 (April 6, 1912): 435.

"From the Social Service Commission," *Universalist Leader*, n.s. 15 (June 15, 1912): 754.

"Social Service Commission," *Universalist Leader*, n.s. 15 (October 5, 1912): 1267.

"One Year of the Social Service Commission," *Universalist Leader*, n.s. 15 (November 16, 1912): 1458.

"Social Service Commission," *Universalist Leader*, n.s. 15 (December 28, 1912): 1648.

"Social Service in Sunday Schools," *Universalist Leader*, n.s. 16 (January 3, 1913): 85-6.

"Report of Social Service Commission," *Universalist Leader*, n.s. 16 (November 8, 1913): 1313-4.

"The Law of Church Life," *Universalist Leader*, n.s. 17 (January 31, 1914): 107.

"The Modern Heretic," *Universalist Leader*, n.s. 17 (January 31, 1914): 111-2.

"Our Social Service Number," *Universalist Leader*, n.s. 17 (January 31, 1914): 107.

"Social Service Fundamental," *Universalist Leader*, n.s. 17 (January 31, 1914): 107-8.

"Church Forum a Means of Interpreting the Life of the Day," *Survey*, 31 (March 14, 1914): 750-1.

"Twentieth Century Universalism. The Social Implications of the Universal Fatherhood of God," *Universalist Leader*, n.s. 17 (May 30, 1914): 519-21.

"The Kingdom of Heaven," *Universalist Leader*, n.s. 18 (February 13, 1915): 147.

"Lowell Social Forum," *Universalist Leader*, n.s. 18 (February 13, 1915): 153-4.

"Social Evangelism," *Universalist Leader*, n.s. 18 (February 13, 1915): 147-8.

"The Social Implications of Universalism: The Challenge," *Universalist Leader*, n.s. 18 (February 13, 1915): 151.

"The Social Implications of Universalism: Freedom," *Universalist Leader*, n.s. 18 (February 20, 1915): 179-80.

"The Social Implications of Universalism: Social Motive," *Universalist Leader*, n.s. 18 (February 27, 1915): 200-1.

"The Social Implications of Universalism: The Leadership of Jesus," *Universalist Leader*, n.s. 18 (March 6, 1915): 226-7.

"The Social Implications of Universalism: God and Democracy," *Universalist Leader*, n.s. 18 (March 13, 1915): 249-51.

"The Social Implications of Universalism: Punishment and Reformation," *Universalist Leader*, n.s. 18 (March 20, 1915): 275-6.

"The Social Implications of Universalism: The New Unity," *Universalist Leader*, n.s. 18 (March 27, 1915): 298-9.

"Has Christianity Failed," *Universalist Leader*, n.s. 19 (January 29, 1916): 100-1.

"Religion and Psychology," *Universalist Leader*, n.s. 18 (September 30, 1916): 886.

"Christ in the School," *Universalist Leader*, n.s. 19 (December 23,1916): 1081.

"The Church and the Forum," *Universalist Leader*, n.s. 20 (May 19, 1917): 316.

"Constructive Universalism," *Universalist Leader,* n.s. 20 (June 9, 1917): 369.

"Religious Reconstruction After the War," *Universalist Leader*, n.s. 20 (October 20, 1917): 697-99.

"The Changing Approach to God," *Universalist Leader*, n.s. 20 (November 17, 1917): 801-3.

"The Changing Idea of God," *Universalist Leader*, n.s. 20 (December 22, 1917): 929-31.

"The Rediscovery of Jesus," *Universalist Leader*, n.s. 21 (March 30, 1918): 265-8.

"Making the World Safe for Religion," *Universalist Leader*, n.s. 21 (April 27, 1918): 349-51.

"The New and the Old," *Universalist Leader*, n.s. 21 (May 4, 1918): 365.

"Faith and the Coming Order," *Universalist Leader*, n.s. 21 (October 26, 1918): 830-2.

"The World Soul," *Universalist Leader*, n.s. 22 (January 11, 1919): 40-1.

"Universalism and Soul of the New Age," *Universalist Leader,* n.s. 22 (January 18, 1919): 55-6.

"What Is a Pacifist?," *Boston Herald*, 28 January 1919.

"Massachusetts Social Service Committee Report," *Universalist Leader*, n.s. 22 (June 21, 1919): 586-7.

"Some Principles of the Future Religion," *Unity*, 83 (July 31, 1919): 259.

"Dr. Powers As a Prophet," *Universalist Leader*, n.s. 24 (February 12, 1921): 183-4.

"The Sacco-Vanzetti Case," *Survey*, 46 (June 25, 1921): 431-2; and 46 (August 16, 1921): 584.

"Loyalty and Co-operation," *Unity*, 8 (January 12, 1922): 277-8.

"The Book of the New Reformation," *Unity*, 89 (April 6, 1922): 85-7 (Review of J. H. Holmes, *New Churches for Old.*).

"An Observation on the Railroad Problem," *Unity*, 89 (May 11, 1922): 167.

"Religion and Freedom," *Unity*, 89 (June 29, 1922): 277-8.

"The Moral Substitute," *Unity*, 89 (July 20, 1922): 313-4.

"America's Superiority Complex," *Unity*, 90 (October 10, 1922): 70-1.

"Are Christians Hypocrites?," *Unity*, 90 (January 4, 1923): 246-7.

"The Church and Social Reform," *Onward*, 30 (February 16, 1923): 4-5.

"A Danger Signal," *Unity*, 91 (March 22, 1923): 54-5.

"Creation Versus Imitation," *Unity*, 91 (June 7, 1923): 230-1.

"Recent Developments in the Sacco-Vanzetti Case," *Unity*, 92 (January 3, 1924): 246-7.

"The Militarist's Fallacy," *Unity*, 92 (January 31, 1924): 312-3.

"Professor Skinner on the Soul," *Universalist Leader*, n.s. 27 (February 2, 1924): 13-4.

"The Church's Stake in the Community," *Onward*, 31 (February 29, 1924): 1-2.

"To the Editor of the Universalist Leader," *Universalist Leader*, n.s. 27 (March 15, 1924): 22-3.

"Religion and Science," *Unity*, 93 (March 20, 1924): 41-2; and 93 (March 27, 1924): 57-9.

"In Times of Disillusion," *Unity*, 93 (April 24, 1924): 119.

"An Open Letter to the War Department of the United States," *Unity*, 93 (June 12, 1924): 233-4.

"Religion and Science: A Psychological Interpretation," *Unity*, 94 (October 16, 1924): 69-72; 94 (October 23, 1924): 85-8; 94 (October 30, 1924): 101-4; 94 (November 6, 1924): 117-9; and 94 (November 13, 1924): 133-6.

"The Dilemma of Racial Judgments," *Unity*, 94 (January 26, 1925): 298.

"Academic Freedom," *Unity*, 96 (October 5, 1925): 37-9.

"To the Warring Sects," *Unity*, 96 (November 16, 1925): 133-4.

"Religion as Experience and Science as Criticism," *Unity*, 96 (January 25, 1926): 293-5; and 96 (February, 1926): 309-12.

"To the Students of America—In Colleges and High Schools," *Unity*, 97 (April 12, 1926): 102.

"Can We Test Ethical Superiority?," *Unity*, 97 (June 14, 1926): 245-6; 97 (June 21, 1926): 261-2; 97 (June 28, 1926): 277-8; 97 (July 5, 1926): 293-4; 97 (July 12, 1926): 310-1; and 97 (July 19, 1926): 326-7.

"Which Will the Christian Church Choose: Christianity Or War?," *Unity*, 98 (January 10, 1927): 294.

"The Drive Against Liberalism in America," *Unity*, 99 (March 7, 1927): 10-5.

"Tempted Radicals," *Unity*, 99 (March 28, 1927): 57-8.

"To the Editor of Unity," *Unity*, 99 (May 16, 1927): 175.

"Superstition, Belief, and Faith," *Unity*, 100 (October 10, 1927): 73-4; 100 (October 17, 1927): 89-91; 100 (October 24, 1927): 105-7; and 100 (October 31, 1927): 121-3.

"Not Capital Punishment—Then What?," *Unity*, 100 (December 26, 1927): 249-50.

"Substitutes for Companionate Marriage," *Unity*, 100 (February 20, 1928): 378-9.

"Intransigent," *Unity*, 101 (March 5, 1928): 27-8.

"Science and Standardized Education," *Unity*, 101 (April 30, 1928): 169-70.

"An Outline for a New College," *Unity*, 102 (November 5, 1928): 125-7; and 102 (November 12, 1928): 141-3.

"It Must Be Done Now!," *Unity*, 102 (January 21, 1929): 301-2.

"Religious Fixations," *Unity*, 103 (April 1, 1929): 69-71; 103 (April 8, 1929): 86-7; and 103 (April 15, 1929): 101-3.

"Sociological Obstacles to Religious Experience," *Unity*, 104 (October 14, 1929): 53-6.

"Rugged Individualism," *Unity*, 104 (January 6, 1930): 245-6.

"Humanism and the Community Church," *Unity*, 105 (March 31, 1930): 69-70.

"Humanism and the Community Church," *Christian Leader*, n.s. 33 (May 17, 1930): 625-6.

"Humanism and the Community Church," *Community Church-man*, 10 (May 1930): 2.

"An Experiment in the Technique of Worship," *Unity*, 105 (June 23, 1930): 261-3. Reprinted as "Explanatory," in *A Free Pulpit in Action*, pp. 1-17.

"Some Neglected Phases of Prejudice," *Unity*, 107 (August 31, 1931): 357-60.

"Psychological Obstacles to Religious Experience," *Unity*, 106 (November 3, 1930): 117-9; 106 (November 10, 1930): 133-5; and 106 (November 17, 1930): 149-51.

"Cycles and Religious Interest," *Unity*, 106 (February 9, 1931): 341-3.

"Danger Ahead," *Unity*, 107 (May 11, 1931): 165-6.

"Notes," *Unity*, 107 (July 20, 1931): 306-7.

"Religion and Revolution," *Christian Leader*, n.s. 34 (November 7, 1931): 1423-4.

"Religious Liberties," *Unity*, 108 (January 4, 1932): 253-6.

"Gandhi and Socialism," *Unity*, 108 (January 25, 1932): 310.

"Motives to Work in a New Social Order," *Unity*, 109 (April 11, 1932): 85-7.

"Economic Planning—Arguments Pro and Con," *Unity*, 109 (August 15, 1932): 325-7.

"Welwyn, England's Latest Garden City," *Unity*, 110 (November 28, 1932): 165-7.

"Dean Skinner to Universalists," *Christian Leader*, n.s. 36 (January 21, 1933): 66, 93-4.

"The Church Faces a New Age," *Christian Leader*, n.s. 36 (March 4, 1933): 262-5.

"The Church Faces a New Age," *Unity*, 111 (March 6, 1933): 5-9.

"Working in the Dark," *Christian Leader*, n.s. 36 (May 27, 1933): 653-4.

"Schweitzer: Saint and Hero," *Unity*, 111 (May 29, 1933): 208-10. (Book review.)

"Preaching the Social Gospel," *Christian Leader*, n.s. 36 (June 3, 1933): 682-5.

"The Humanist Manifesto," *Unity*, 111 (June 12, 1933): 233-5.

"Snap-Shots of Russia," *Unity*, 112 (September 4, 1933): 7-9; and 112 (September 18, 1933): 23-6.

"This Revolutionary Age," *Christian Leader*, n.s. 37 (December 1, 1934): 1510-2; and n.s. 37 (December 8, 1934): 1545-7.

"Prejudice: An Instinct, a Conditioning, or a Purpose?," *Unity*, 116 (January 6, 1936): 166-7.

"Experimentation with Definite Goals," *Christian Register*, 115 (April 30, 1936): 297.

"Experimentation with Definite Goals," *Christian Leader*, n.s. 39 (May 2, 1936): 560-1.

"Function of Liberalism in a World of Rising Authorities: What Is Liberalism?," *Christian Leader*, n.s. 39 (October 17, 1936): 1318-20.

"Function of Liberalism in a World of Rising Authorities: The Roots of Modern Liberalism," *Christian Leader*, n.s. 39 (October 24, 1936): 1350-3.

"Function of Liberalism in a World of Rising Authorities: The Development of Liberalism," *Christian Leader*, n.s. 39 (November 7, 1936): 1418-20; and n.s. 39 (November 14, 1936): 1455-8.

"Function of Liberalism in a World of Rising Authorities: A Philosophy of Liberalism," *Christian Leader*, n.s. 39 (November 21, 1936): 1478-80; and n.s. 39 (December 19, 1936): 1608-11.

"Function of Liberalism in a World of Rising Authorities: The Weakness of Liberalism," *Christian Leader*, n.s. 40 (January 2, 1937): 11-15.

"Function of Liberalism in a World of Rising Authorities: The World of Rising Authoritarianism," *Christian Leader*, n.s. 40 (February 6, 1937): 168-72.

"Function of Liberalism in a World of Rising Authorities: New Horizons for Liberalism," *Christian Leader*, 119 (February 27, 1937): 270-2; 119 (March 27, 1937); and 119 (April 10, 1937): 454-6.

"Dr. Skinner's Prayer, Goddard Chapel, July Fifth, Nineteen Thirty-Seven," *Tufts College Alumni Bulletin*, 11 (December, 1937): no page given.

"Worship," *Christian Leader,* 120 (April 16, 1938): 490.

"Alumni Hall at Tufts College School of Religion," *Christian Leader*, 120 (July 9, 1938): 870.

"Social Implications of Universalism," *Helper*, 70 (January, 1939): 3-43.

"What Religion Means to Me," *Christian Leader*, 121 (February 18, 1939): 154-6. Also in Tufts Papers on Religion, 7-16.

"The Nature of Evil," *Journal of Liberal Religion,* 1 (Autumn 1939): 19-26. (Chapter III of *Human Nature and the Nature of Evil.*)

"Why I Am Still a Pacifist," *Unity*, 124 (November 6, 1939): 70-1.

"Fifty-Seven Varieties," *Christian Leader*, 121 (December 30, 1939): 1244-5.

"Theology and Sociology," *Journal of Liberal Religion*, 1 (Winter 1940): 49-50. (Book review.)

"Tufts College School of Religion," *Christian Leader*, 122 (May 11, 1940): 473-74.

"Our Prodigal Son Culture," *Christian Leader*, 122 (September 14, 1940): 810.

"The Family and Childhood of John Murray," (with A. S. Cole) *Christian Leader*, 123 (March 1, 1941): 198-200; and 123 (March 8, 1941): 221-3.

"Growing Up in Ireland" (with A. S. Cole), *Christian Leader*,

123 (March 15, 1941): 246-8; and 123 (March 22, 1941): 274-6.

"England: The Highest Happiness and the Deepest Despair" (with A. S. Cole), *Christian Leader*, 123 (March 29, 1941): 300-3; and 123 (April 5, 1941): 321-3.

"Good Luck" (with A. S. Cole), *Christian Leader*, 123 (April 12, 1941): 348-9; and 123 (April 19, 1941): 367-9.

"The American Background" (with A. S. Cole), *Christian Leader*, 123 (May 3, 1941): 397-8; and 123 (May 10, 1941): 414-6.

"Man on Horseback" (with A. S. Cole), *Christian Leader*, 123 (May 31, 1941): 459-61; and 123 (June 7, 1941): 476-7.

"Beginnings at Gloucester" (with A. S. Cole), *Christian Leader*, 123 (June 21, 1941): 507-9.

"Gloucester and the Chaplaincy" (with A. S. Cole), *Christian Leader*, 123 (July 5, 1941): 539-41.

"The End: Evaluation" (with A. S. Cole), *Christian Leader*, 123 (August 16, 1941): 635-8.

"The Implications of Murray's Universalism for the World of Today" (with A. S. Cole), *Christian Leader*, 123 (September 13, 1941): 718.

"Reminiscences of Otis Skinner," *Christian Leader*, 124 (February 7, 1942): 73-4.

"Worship," *Onward*, 49 (June 1943): 1.

"Will Truth Make Us Free?," *Christian Leader*, 125 (July 3, 1943): 390-3.

"A Religion for Greatness: Radical Religion," *Christian Leader*, 125 (December 4, 1943): 710-3.

"A Religion for Greatness: Religion of the Unities and the Universals," *Christian Leader*, 125 (December 18, 1943): 744-8.

"A Religion for Greatness: Examples," *Christian Leader*, 126 (January 1, 1944): 19-21.

"A Religion for Greatness: When Men Are More Than Men," *Christian Leader*, 126 (January 15, 1944): 50-1.

"A Religion for Greatness: Economic Universalism," *Christian*

Leader, 126 (February 5, 1944): 79-81; and 126 (February 19, 1944): 106-9.

"A Religion for Greatness: Racial Universalism," *Christian Leader*, 126 (March 4, 1944): 139-43; and 126 (March 18, 1944): 173-5.

"Communion Service for Youth," *Onward*, 50 (Lenten Issue, 1944): 4.

"A Religion for Greatness: Political Universalism," *Christian Leader*, 126 (April 15, 1944): 232-5; and 126 (May 6, 1944): 268-71.

"A Religion for Greatness: Social Universalism," *Christian Leader*, 126 (May 20, 1944): 300-3.

"A Religion for Greatness: Scientific Universalism," *Christian Leader*, 126 (September 2, 1944): 524-6; and 126 (October 7, 1944): 582-5.

"The Social Action Commission of the Universalist Church of America," *Christian Leader*, 127 (February 3, 1945): 61-2.

"The President, a Memorial Service," *Tuftonian*, 5 (Spring 1945): 6-10. (Contains Skinner's invocation and benediction.)

"Dr. Wolfe's Fine Book," *Christian Leader*, 127 (July 1945): 306.

"Choosing a Way of Life," *Young Liberal*, 1 (October 1945): 3-4, 19.

"Prejudice, What It Is and What It Does," *Christian Leader*, 128 (February 2, 1946): 57-8, 61.

"Universalism vs. Partialism," *Bay State Universalist*, 1 (December 1946): 1.

"Superstition, Reason and Faith," *Christian Leader*, 128 (November 16, 1946): 521-4; and 128 (December 7, 1946): 549-52. Reprinted in *Voices of Liberalism*: 2, Boston: Beacon Press, 1948, pp. 203-30.

"Can Religion Solve Our Problems?," *Christian Leader*, 130 (February 21, 1948): 77-80.

"The World of Tomorrow," *Christian Leader*, 130 (June 19, 1948): 269-71.

"Inner Resources," *Christian Leader*, 132 (August 1950): 272-4.

"The Church As a Universalist Community," *Edge*, 1 (1954) No. 2: 1-32.

"Liberalism and Worship," *Edge*, 1 (1955) No. 3: 5-12.

Universalist Trumpet, 12 (May 1958): 1. (Untitled quote from *Worship and a Well Ordered Life*.)

PAMPHLETS

"Choosing a Way of Life," Boston: Universalist Church of America, [1946?].

"Clarence Russell Skinner Speaks," Boston: Unitarian Universalist Association Pamphlet Commission Publication, 1986. (Selections by James D. Hunt, Edited by Daniel G. Higgins, Jr.)

"Ethics, Philosophy and Religion," Boston: Community Church of Boston, January 17, 1932. (Symposium with Edgar S. Brightman and Johannes F. Auer.)

"Superstition, Reason and Faith," Boston: Universalist Publishing House, 1926.

"Testing for Ethical Superiority," Boston: Community Church, [1926].

"Will Truth Make Us Free?," Boston: Universalist Publishing House, n.d.

BIOGRAPHY AND CRITICISM ABOUT SKINNER

Bowen, Patricia M. "The Humiliati of Tufts." Thesis for Meadville/Lombard Theological School, Chicago, 1978.

Cole, Alfred S. "Clarence R. Skinner, Prophet of the Larger Faith," *Universalist Leader*, 143 (April 1961): 75-6, 80.

____. "Clarence Skinner: Prophet of Twentieth Century Universalism." Boston: Universalist Historical Society, 1956.

____. "Prophet of Twentieth Century Universalism," *Universalist Leader*, 136 (November 1955): 263-8.

Gaines, Charles A. "Clarence R. Skinner: The Dark Years," *Annual Journal of the Universalist Historical Society*, 3 (1962): 1-13.

_____. "Clarence R. Skinner: Image of a Movement," Church History research thesis, Crane Theological School, 1961.

Howe, Charles A. *The Larger Faith*. Boston: Skinner House, 1993. (See especially pp. 92-8.)

_____. "The Universalist Vision: Its History and Significance," in *Regaining Historical Consciousness, Proceedings of the Earl Morse Wilbur History Colloquium*, Berkeley: Starr King School, 1994. (See pp. 55-6.)

Hunt, James D. "Introduction" to the reprint of *The Social Implications of Universalism, Annual Journal of the Universalist Historical Society,* 5 (1964-65): 79-8. (Reprinted by the Universalist Historical Society and Beacon Press as number 4 in the Beacon Reference Series, pp. 5-14, 1966.)

_____. "The Liberal Theology of Clarence R. Skinner," *Annual Journal of the Universalist Historical Society*, 7 (1967-68): 102-20.

Joughin, George Louis, and Morgan, Edmund M. *The Legacy of Sacco and Vanzetti*. New York: Harcourt, Brace, 1948. (See pp. 226-7, 238.)

Low, A. Ritchie. "A Liberal Looks at Life: An Interview with Dean Clarence R. Skinner of Tufts," *Christian Leader*, 125 (November 20, 1943): 692-4.

Miller, Russell E. "A History of Universalist Theological Education," *Proceedings of the Unitarian Universalist Historical Society*, Vol. XX - Part I:1-94, 1984. (See pp. 54-70.)

_____. *The Larger Hope: The Second Century of the Universalist Church in America, 1870-1970*. Boston: Unitarian Universalist Association, 1985. (See the index, footnotes, and especially pp. 318-9 and 496-509.)

_____. *Light on the Hill: A History of Tufts College, 1852-1952*. Boston: Beacon Press, 1966. (See especially pp. 539-40 and 664-65.)

Patton, Kenneth L. "Introduction," *Edge*, 1, No. 2 (1954): ii, 33-4.

Pennington, George J. W. "Universalist Interpretations." Senior thesis 32, Tufts College School of Religion, 1947. (See pp. 72-4.)

Robinson, David. "Skinner, Clarence Russell," in *The Unitarians and the Universalists*. Westport, Conn.: Greenwood, 1985. (See pp. 7, 139-41, 172, 321-2.)

Scott, Clinton Lee. *These Live Tomorrow*. Boston: Beacon, 1964. (See pp. 253-64.)

Seaburg, Carl. "Clarence Skinner: Building a New Kind of Church," in *To Bring More Light and Understanding*, the John Murray Distinguished Lectures, Vol. 2, Edited by Charles A. Howe. Lanoka Harbor, NJ: Murray Grove Association, 1995. (See pp. 49-69.)

_____. "Skinner, Clarence Russell," in *American National Biography*. New York: Oxford, 1998.

Voss, Carl Hermann. *Rabbi and Minister: The Friendship of Stephen S. Wise and John Haynes Holmes*. New York: Association, 1964. (See p. 174.)

Williams, George Huntston. *American Universalism. Annual Journal of the Universalist Historical Society*, 9 (1971): 1-94. (See especially pp. 56-7 and 83-4.) Reprinted as *American Universalism: A Bicentennial Essay*. Boston: Skinner House Books, 1976.

REVIEWS OF SKINNER'S BOOKS

A Free Pulpit in Action

Brown, C. S. *Survey*, 66 (May 15, 1931): 235.

Brummitt, Dan. *Christian Century*, 48 (February 4,1931): 173.

Hussey, Alfred R. *Christian Register*, 110 (March 19, 1931): 235.

Parrish, Herbert. *Books* (July 12, 1931): p. 8.

R., T. C. *Boston Transcript* (February 11, 1931): 3.

Trout, John M. *Christian Leader,* n.s. 34 (February 28, 1931): 285.

Liberalism Faces the Future
Argow, W. Waldemar W. *Unity*, 120 (February 21, 1938): 194-5.
C. H. *Churchman*, 152 (March 1, 1938): 34.
Bixler, J. S. *Harvard Divinity School Bulletin*, 35 (April 1, 1938): 100.
Booklist, 34 (December 1, 1937): 127.
Case, S. J. *Journal of Religion*, 18 (July 1938): 372.
Christian Century, 55 (December 7, 1938): 1509.
Foreign Affairs, 16 (April 1938): 542.
Palyi, Melchior. *American Journal of Sociology,* 44 (September 1938): 315.
Pittenger, W. N. *Living Church*, 99 (October 19, 1938): 384.
Powell, E. W. *Crozer Quarterly*, 15 (January 1938): 49.
Speight, Harold E. B. *Christian Leader*, 119 (November 6, 1937): 1434.
Times (London) Literary Supplement (April 16, 1938): 267.

Human Nature and the Nature of Evil
Atwood, John Murray. *Christian Leader*, 121 (December 16, 1939): 1206.
Churchman, 154 (March 1, 1940): 35.
Holmes, J. H. *Books* (December 24, 1939): 11.
MacPherson, W. H. *Journal of Liberal Religion,* 1 (Spring 1940): 51-2.

Hell's Ramparts Fell
Christian Century, 58 (November 19, 1941): 1443.
L.,T. L. *Christian Science Monitor* (February 14, 1942): 12.
Weis, Frederick L. *Journal of Liberal Religion,* 4 (Summer 1942): 55-6.

A Religion for Greatness
  Cole, Alfred S. *Christian Leader*, 127 (August 4, 1945): 348.

Worship and a Well Ordered Life
  Lalone, Emerson H. *Universalist Leader*, 138 (January 1956): 18.
  Schwarzschild, Steven S. *Judaism*, 10 (Summer 1961): 277.

OBITUARIES

"Clarence Russell Skinner," *Christian Leader*, 131 (October 1949): 344.
"God's Unsurrendered: A Tribute to Clarence R. Skinner," *Christian Leader*, 131 (October 1949): 348-52.
New York Times (August 28, 1949): 73.
School and Society, 70 (September 3, 1949): 159.
"Skinner Memorial Service Opening John Hancock Hall," *Community Church News*, October 1949.
Tufts Alumni Review, 4 (Fall 1949): 41.

Index